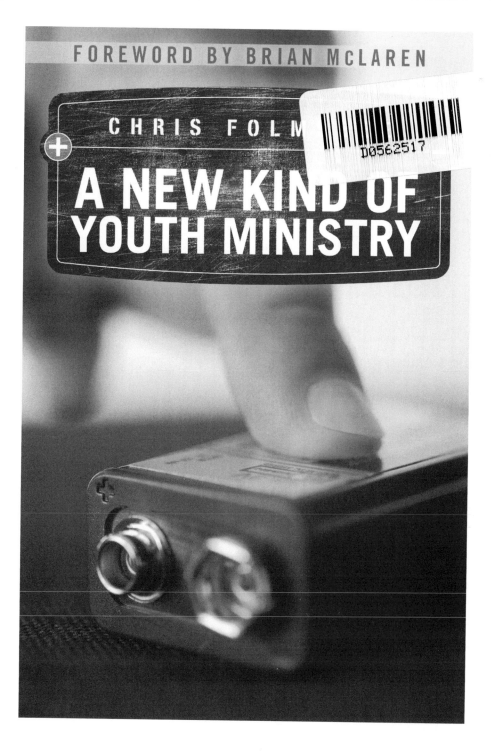

FOREWORD BY BRIAN McLAREN

CHRIS FOLM

A NEW KIND OF
YOUTH MINISTRY

D0562517

ZONDERVAN®

Youth Specialties
.com

ZONDERVAN.com/
AUTHORTRACKER
follow your favorite authors

Youth Specialties

A New Kind of Youth Ministry
Copyright © 2007 by Chris Folmsbee

Youth Specialties products, 300 S. Pierce St., El Cajon, CA 92020 are published by Zondervan, 5300 Patterson Ave. SE, Grand Rapids, MI 49530.

Library of Congress Cataloging-in-Publication Data

Folmsbee, Chris.
  A new kind of youth ministry / By Chris Folmsbee.
      p. cm.
  Includes bibliographical references and index.
  ISBN-10: 0-310-26989-X (pbk. : alk. paper)
  ISBN-13: 978-0-310-26989-2 (pbk. : alk. paper)
  1. Church work with youth. I. Title.
  BV4447.F66 2006
  259'.23--dc22

                                                                      2006024008

This edition printed on acid-free paper.

All Scripture quotations, unless otherwise indicated, are taken from the *Holy Bible: New International Version*®. NIV®. Copyright © 1973, 1978, 1984 by International Bible Society. Used by permission of Zondervan. All rights reserved.

All rights reserved. No part of this publication may be reproduced, stored in a retrieval system, or transmitted in any form or by any means—electronic, mechanical, photocopy, recording, or any other—except for brief quotations in printed reviews, without the prior permission of the publisher.

Web site addresses listed in this book were current at the time of publication. Please contact Youth Specialties via e-mail (YS@YouthSpecialties.com) to report URLs that are no longer operational and replacement URLs if available.

Creative Team: Doug Davidson, Brad Taylor, Heather Haggerty, Mark Novelli/IMAGO MEDIA
Cover Design by Toolbox Studios

Printed in the United States of America

06 07 08 09 10 11 12 • 23 22 21 20 19 18 17 16 15 14 13 12 11 10 9 8 7 6 5 4 3 2 1

All my heart and thanks to:

Gina

Megan, Drew, & Luke

Thanks, Gina, for your love, friendship, and support.

⊕ CONTENTS

⊕ FOREWORD

If I could do it over again, there's a good chance I would do youth ministry. It's not because I think young people are "the church of tomorrow." It's because I think they're the church of today that will last longer!

It's also because youth workers get an amazing opportunity: to model Christian living—potentially *radical* Christian living—for young people who are actually in search of models for how their lives can be. (Too often, in "older adult ministry," the conventional pastor ends up serving as what Tom Beaudoin has called a "sacramental grace dispenser"–a human Pez dispenser who meets the needs of discriminating [read "finicky"] consumers of religious products and services.)

If I got to start over again as a youth worker, I'm not sure I'd use the term "youth ministry" to describe what I was doing. I sometimes think "youth ministry" should apply to preadolescents, and we should call teenagers–in the Jewish tradition of bar mitzvah and bat mitzvah–young adults. So maybe I'd call it "young adult ministry." Even better, I might call it "disciple-making ministry," or even better–I wouldn't call it anything, just life.

Anyway, if I got to start over again, I would want to learn all I could from Chris Folmsbee. When I get discouraged with the state of religion in America and beyond, I think of people like Chris, and the tide of hope comes in again.

The book you're holding provides a fine introduction to Chris and his perspective. I believe you'll find it clear and practical–two adjectives without which the book wouldn't be read by many people. But it's what goes beyond "clear" and "practical" that most impressed me as I read *A New Kind of Youth Ministry.*

First, the book is sincere. Chris isn't trying to impress you or make a name for himself. He cares about teenagers. He is committed to Jesus Christ as Lord. And he knows these two great commitments go together. His sincere desire to see young people become authentic followers of Jesus gives this book something that goes far beyond the typical hype and excitement.

This leads to a second quality of Chris' work: It is honest. Chris is too serious about disciple-making among young people to tiptoe around bad ideas and sacred cows. He questions some pretty settled assumptions and raises some difficult questions and doesn't coddle anyone's denial about the depth of the challenges we face in doing authentic Christian ministry in these times.

In addition to sincere and honest, I think you'll find this book is also bold and solid. It's not cotton candy or whipped cream. It's meat and potatoes or, for vegetarians, it's handpicked fruit and vegetables from Chris's own garden.

One other thing. The book is incomplete. It's not the last word or the ultimate solution. Nor should it (or any book) pretend to be. It left me thinking, "This is really good. So good, in fact, that I can't wait to hear what else Chris will have to say a few years down the road." I think you'll feel the same way. I think you'll share my belief that Chris is a young leader we'll be watching and learning from for years to come.

You're a youth worker, I assume, or a friend of a youth worker. Reading this book will be good for you. And that reminds me of one other thing I want to tell you: Because youth ministry is so important, I hope you'll take care of yourself. I know people say, "There's no I in team." But maybe we should start spelling it "teim" or something. Because the fact is, your team will suffer if you aren't experiencing ongoing growth and personal development.

So, because your work is so important, and because you're important, take care of your soul and stay close to God—not just because you're getting paid for it, but because that's what life's about, and that's who you are: a close-to-God person. Take care of your emotions and stay in touch with yourself and with some friends who know how to practice peer mentoring and mutual encouragement. Of course, take care of your body and get enough sleep, rest, and exercise. And please, take care of your mind. What you're doing demands the hard work of real thought and continual learning—not just a ratrace of wild and crazy activities.

Reading this book can be a wise step in taking care of your mind. And that will be good for you, and your team, and the young people whose lives you touch. In fact, even the as-yet unborn (and unimagined) grandchildren of your young people may benefit in some way from the thinking and learning you'll engage in when you turn the next page.

When you turn the last page, I think you'll join me in thanking Chris for this clear, practical, sincere, honest, solid, and bold book.

— Brian McLaren

PREFACE

Before you leap into the pages of this book, you should know several things. First, even though this book is all about changing the way we do youth ministry, please know that I have deep admiration and respect for those who have come before me in this field. If it were not for people like Mike Yaconelli, Pamela Erwin, Doug Fields, and others who paved the way for those of us who do ministry with students, I don't know where I'd be. Throughout this book I've tried not to disparage the last several decades of youth ministry. Without apology, however, I've tried to rethink many of the customs, beliefs, and precedents of modern youth ministry. I'm not suggesting we need to change our style of ministry merely because it is old, but because of the rapid pace of cultural change around us. I believe what we've been doing for the last several decades is no longer effective, and will grow less and less effective in the coming days.

Second, you should know that I am not an academic. You won't find tons of exacting data and verified clinical studies to measure the effectiveness of the approach to ministry in this book. I like to think in new ways and to be pushed by the creative ideas of others, but I do not consider myself a scholar. Calling me an academic or a scholar is like calling me a golfer. I like to play golf, but I'm not a golfer. A golfer goes out and hits fairways and greens, makes putts, and walks into the clubhouse for a frosty or two with a score somewhere near par. On the other hand, I'm a hacker on the golf course who might score below 90 on a good day. So while I like to play golf and can even play with the golfers, I am not one of them. In the same light, I am not a scholar. I consider scholars in the youth ministry world to be people like Tony Jones of Emergent, Kenda Dean of Princeton Theological Seminary, Mike King of YouthFront, David White of Austin Seminary, Dave Livermore and Steve Argue of Intersect Community, and Pamela Erwin of Bethel University. I can sit with these folks over coffee and talk about ideas that might shape the future of youth ministry. But at the end of the day, I am a practitioner—one who takes the highly specialized and theoretical ideas of others and experiments with them expectantly, waiting and watching for beneficial and transferable outcomes.

This book is the product of who I am as a practitioner. It's filled with ideas and practices that I've sweated through, cried through, laughed through, lost my temper through, learned through, been surprised by, and been shaped by. I'm glad to say that my own ministry has recognized many positive outcomes from the ideas in this book. But I don't have an easy step-by-step plan for success.

Throughout the book you will find boxes that offer you information about groups that are doing youth ministry in new and exciting ways. Each of these includes a Web address where you can learn more about the featured ministry. The information about these groups can serve as an inspiration and a resource to you as you think about how your own ministry can grow and change to meet the needs of this new day. I've also included questions for discussion and reflection at the end of each chapter. I hope these questions will help you and your ministry team consider more carefully how the insights in this book apply to your own ministry context.

Finally, you should know that *A New Kind of Youth Ministry* is not as much about new *inventions* and *innovations* in ministry as it is about our biblically based *intentions* as caretakers of our student communities. *A New Kind of Youth Ministry* is rooted in a commitment to the youth of today—a generation that needs you and me to critically assess all we've come to know about youth ministry so we can selectively and intentionally incorporate new ideas and practices that will help our students deepen their relationships with God.

INTRODUCTION

My Journey toward a New Kind of Youth Ministry

I hadn't been a full-time youth worker for very long before I was having questions about the most effective way to make disciples of teenagers. During my college days and over an in-depth two-year internship, I'd been taught a traditional model of youth ministry—a model built largely around events, fellowship activities, Sunday school, and service projects. I knew such an approach had its positive elements. But within a few months of taking my first full-time youth ministry position, I sensed students were becoming increasingly disinterested in an event-based model. The more new events we organized and produced, the more we tried to enhance our programming, the more I observed our ministry's inability to help teens connect with God authentically. Early into my ministry life, I began to crave, pray for and hope for a new kind of youth ministry.

Not knowing what to do with this craving, I reluctantly continued to do youth ministry the way I'd been trained. I organized outreach events to connect with unbelievers, I produced discipleship-oriented programs to help students grow in their faith, and I trained students with the necessary skill sets and involved them in the work of the ministry. But all the while I knew ministry to youth could look and feel much different. I struggled to find the words to communicate my desire for another kind of youth ministry. Yet my conversations with other youth workers and church leaders about "new ways" usually left me feeling increasingly frustrated with the efforts of the church—and left others feeling equally frustrated with me.

Irritated, discontented, and restless, I hopped from church to church, thinking each new location would be a better place for me to do youth ministry. In my frequent transitions, I was eager to find a church that would let me experiment with new ideas and practices. At the time, however, I was unable to locate a church (or even another youth pastor, for that matter) that was even thinking about doing youth ministry in a new way. I'm sure there were others out there who were envisioning a different model of youth ministry—maybe you were one of them. For whatever reason, I couldn't find you. I ran into many other youth workers striving to "make more and better disciples" by refining and building upon what was already being done. But I found very few who were looking to do ministry in a completely different way. Most youth workers I met seemed content with enhancing the ordinary way.

For many youth pastors, the traditional model did "work"—and it's hard to protest against what works or seemingly works. Parents and church leaders want results. They want to know that the money they place in the offering plate each week is being used well and that students' lives are changing for the better. I can't blame them for that. In fact, my own desire to see results by the traditional measures— growth in numbers, changes in behavior, and church participation—was one reason I felt afraid to pursue a new kind of ministry. What if we tried something different and it didn't work? Would I be considered a failure? Would I lose my job? And yet I knew that having more kids at an event doesn't always mean young people are becoming passionate followers of Jesus.

Not long after making a decision to move to yet another church, I picked up a book that would push me past my fears and pride and encourage me to experiment with a new kind of youth ministry at all costs. In Tony Jones' book *Postmodern Youth Ministry* (Zondervan, 2001), I was encouraged to find someone who was thinking about and doing youth ministry in a new way! Tony was a lot further down the road than I was in his discoveries, and he was able to articulate well the very things I hadn't yet put into words. But I deeply resonated with *Postmodern Youth Ministry*, particularly statements like this:

> Evangelism (proclaiming the Good News) and Apologetics (defending the faith) must always be done in culturally appropriate ways. And in a world in which absolute, foundational truth is being overthrown in fields like mathematics, physics, philosophy, and language theory, it seems ludicrous that Christians would insist that ours is the one indubitably sure thing in the world.

I resonated with Tony's words, not because of their edginess or even the controversial conversations they often inspired, but because they echoed the questions I was hearing from students. I was working every day with youth who had no real reason *not* to follow Jesus, just a lot of questions about what it meant to follow him. Tony spoke directly to the idea and questions I was hearing from the mouths and hearts of students. Until interacting with Tony's book, I'd had no idea what to think about the issues my students were raising—let alone how to respond to them.

I contacted Tony, and he was kind enough to meet with me. With Tony's help, I began to get my arms around postmodernism and my responsibility to develop a new way to think about and exercise ministry to youth. Tony mentored me—giving me books to read, thoughts to consider, and new paradigms for the art of youth ministry.

I began reading every book on postmodernism and the emerging church I could get my hands on. I was reading two books a week, even in the midst of a full-time job and finishing up a graduate degree. I just couldn't get enough of Brian McLaren, Stan Grenz, Doug Pagitt, Len Sweet—anyone who was writing on the topic of postmodern culture and the church's response to it. Their work pushed me to dig into the writings of people like St. John of the Cross, Brother Lawrence, and Thomas à Kempis. I was fully entrenched in the lives, theologies, and ministries of authors I'd not only never read before, but often had never even heard of.

These writings caused me to rethink everything I thought I knew—my theological framework, the role of the church, the conversion experience, my own spirituality, leadership models, worship, social justice issues, and a host of youth ministry basics like evangelism, discipleship, ministry training, and programming techniques. I finally decided I had no choice but to revise my whole approach to youth ministry.

At the time I was the pastor of student ministries at a megachurch with a long heritage of "successful" youth ministry. Soon our ministry team began the arduous journey that author Michael Fullan refers to as *reculturing*. Reculturing is a strategic and intentional process of change that involves concentrated critical assessment, passionate idea generation, implementation of new ideas and practices, and the ongoing evaluation of effectiveness of the changes implemented. In his book *Leading in a Culture of Change* (Jossey-Bass, 2001), Fullan notes that reculturing "does not mean adopting innovations one after another; it does mean producing the capacity to seek, critically assess, and selectively incorporate new ideas and practices."

Reculturing is not a one-time deal. Instead, it is an ever-developing ethos of change that will allow us to effectively navigate the fluidity of our ministry contexts. According to Fullan, reculturing is "a contact sport"—in other words, like football, it involves teamwork, player roles, practice, pain, sweat, injury, error, celebration, success, a playbook, and a coach or two. Reculturing is not for the weary or faint of heart. It takes a willingness to leave behind all that is comfortable and certain and risk journeying in a new direction—not so much for your sake as for the sake of all whom you are called to influence.

Along with my ministry team, I began to lead change by incorporating new ideas, practices, and ministry paradigms. Together, our team transformed nearly every part of our work with youth. We moved from a teacher- and curriculum-based educational model to a learner-based model. We created new opportunities for spiritual formation. We developed a new teaching emphasis on social justice issues, calling students to a way of life that took them beyond themselves and encouraging them to live out the virtues of Jesus. We began training in concepts like life-dynamic evangelism and missional living. We made a new commitment to helping students see their role as agents of God's restoring grace and love. We inspired students to find themselves within the grand story of God and then, in turn, become storytellers, thereby moving toward a larger and more comprehensive understanding of the gospel. We moved away from prioritizing programs and encouraged volunteers to think of themselves not as people who run errands to keep a program going but as spiritual directors in the lives of students.

We encouraged staff and leaders to first think theologically as they considered every aspect of youth ministry. And we paid more careful attention to our own spiritual lives, not just the lives of the students. (After all, what good is a disciple-making ministry led by people who are not concerned with their own spiritual lives?)

Everything became new and different. It wasn't change just for the sake of change, but change aimed toward achieving maximum impact in the lives of our youth. Students were engaging more deeply with God and one another. Conversations went from the trivial to the theological. And students were sharing their stories of growth within a community characterized by a renewed sense of compassion, inclusiveness, and kingdom-oriented actions. Our ministry was transforming—and so were our students and leaders!

Around this time I started a ministry called The Trek Project which would allow me to begin consulting with other churches and youth ministries that had a passion for doing youth ministry in new ways. The Trek Project gave me a chance to help other leaders and churches respond to the maturing beliefs of the emerging generations. Not only were we seeing changes in the ministry at our congregation, we were seeing exciting new directions in youth ministries across the country.

But true transformation is never an easy process. About a year into the reculturing process at our church, we were teaching a method of allowing the Bible to shape your life called *lectio divina*. It's an ancient monastic practice characterized by a slow, contemplative praying of the Scriptures, which enables the Bible, the Word of God, to become a means of union with God. Even though students were showing up after school to pray and read Scripture together, *lectio divina* was new, unfamiliar, and somewhat threatening to many of our parents. I readily admit that I didn't do a great job of proactively communicating with parents and church leaders about the changes we were making. (Much of what I know now about leading has come from mistakes I've made!) Before long, parents freaked—and our practice of *lectio divina* became a focal point for questioning all we were doing in the youth ministry.

In the wake of this crisis, my wife and I realized that the parents in this congregation were no longer welcoming us to speak into the lives of their children. The angry phone calls, anonymous letters, and my repeatedly being described as a "new-age spiritualist" were making my worst fears a reality—I was indirectly being asked to step down as the youth pastor. After months of meetings and forums with parents and church leaders, my wife and I concluded we were being called to move on to what God had next.

We hated leaving that church. We loved the students and volunteer leaders. My wife and I had deep friendships with some of my staff and their families. It had been our first experience of authentic community. But we did not want to cause further division within the church. So after many conversations with mentors and other godly people, and a ton of prayer, I resigned.

The time after leaving my position at the church was extremely hard on me. It took me awhile to recognize that God was preparing me for something different. I wasn't quite sure where God was leading my family and me, but I became more and more convinced that I was being called to be a voice of change in youth ministry. I continued consulting with other churches, speaking at forums and conferences, and dialoguing with other youth pastors across North America. And everywhere I went, I saw evidence of the need for a new kind of youth ministry. Here's what I was encountering:

- Few youth pastors I knew were satisfied with the current state of youth ministry. While they could create programs that convinced parents and church leaders their ministries were effective, they knew that it was becoming increasingly difficult to help this generation of students to develop as followers of Jesus.

- Everywhere I went youth ministers were talking about the need for change in youth ministry. But very few were actually putting a reculturing strategy in place.

- Many churches and church leaders were fervently seeking ways to reach the changing culture, but didn't know how to do so.

- Many church leaders and parents were freaked out by the word *postmodern*, associating it with concepts like deconstructionalism and the loss of absolute truth. Often, these well-intentioned folks had no idea what the word really meant. But somewhere along the way, they'd heard that *postmodern* was bad, so they concluded that using it in the same sentence with the words *youth ministry* couldn't be a good thing.

- There was a serious and ever-widening chasm of misunderstanding within the church between those who supported emerging ministry and those who were wary of emerging approaches. I was seeing not only a divergence in ministry philosophies but also strong dislike and sometimes even hatred toward those with the opposing view. Youth pastors who wanted to pursue a more emergent approach to ministry often had to leave their established youth ministry and plant a new church in order to put these new ideas into practice.

THE ASCENT
Ty Wilson
www.theascentonline.com

The Ascent is a Christ-centered, cross-denominational, community ministry for the youth of Golden, Colorado. Rooted in a three-fold understanding of Matthew 4:19—"Come, follow, go"—the Ascent's mission is to grow seasoned climbers for Christ. The ministry includes Baptist, Presbyterian, Lutheran, Episcopal, and nondenominational churches, and is led by the youth pastors of these congregations. Students from these congregations meet together weekly, share stories in small groups, participate in corporate worship, laugh and play games, and serve others together. They are functioning together within a new kind of youth ministry!

Director Ty Wilson says that the adult volunteers in the Ascent work, pray, and train together. They take part in the same mission trips and parents meetings. (Yes, the parents from First Baptist attend the same meeting as parents from Faith Lutheran!) The fundraising is also shared, with the money being allocated in a central account. They have one database, one health waiver, and one Lord and Savior!

- Many churches were responding in a reactionary way to the possibility of change, often by becoming more conservative and fundamentalist in their behavior. Some churches seemed to believe they already had all the theological answers, and the only way to protect their correct views from being infiltrated was to build a wall of protection and keep out everyone with different ideas and assumptions.

- Students and young people were being inaccurately linked to all manner of evil because of fears rooted in a misunderstanding of postmodernism. Some of the statements about today's teens that I heard from church leaders and parents were absolutely shocking. It was as if these adults had given up on the current generation. When referring to the youth of today, their comments were full of disgust, disbelief, and despair, rather than faith, hope, and love.

As I observed the condition of youth ministry across North America, it felt more and more clear to me that we needed to rethink the way churches were doing youth ministry. I felt more and more clear that God was placing in my heart a renewed passion and commitment to helping others think about how to practice a new kind of youth ministry.

When I was speaking at a conference a few weeks ago, I was asked, "So, what does a new kind of youth ministry look like? How will you know when your dreams come true?" Great questions. I'll know we are functioning within a new kind of youth ministry when we experience things like:

- Churches embracing youth ministry in a postmodern culture with optimism and hope instead of pessimism and despair.

- Churches working together cooperatively within their communities regardless of denomination or doctrinal differences in order to develop followers of Jesus who share in God's mission.

- Youth workers seeing themselves primarily as spiritual directors rather than program directors.

- Youth ministries thinking theologically before methodologically.

- Students living out the story of God's restorative mission, not just talking about it.

- Youth workers serving students in cooperation with families and churches rather than in conflict with them.

- Students seeking continually to become more holy today than they were yesterday.

- Church leaders from the "old school" and the "new school" working together in ministry without regard to personal preferences, styles, and the need to be right.

- Youth ministries teaching for spiritual formation rather than for the retaining of information.

- The inventions and innovations of youth workers taking a back seat to their biblical intentions in nurturing a student community.

- Community being seen as not only an aspiration of our ministries but as something practiced within our ministries.

- Students dreaming God-sized dreams and seeing themselves as uniquely gifted contributors to God's mission—whether they see themselves as "leaders" or not.

- Parents understanding their own role in the formation of

CHRIST COMMUNITY CHURCH
Jim Newberry/Alan Mercer
www.cccstudents.com

The leaders of the student ministry at Christ Community Church in Leawood, Kansas, know it is critical to encourage and challenge parents to play a central role in the spiritual formation of their children. Jim Newberry's greeting letter to parents of his high school ministry reads, "We view the family as being the primary spiritually shaping influence in a student's life, and our role is to come alongside you and support you in that role. We realize there will be times that we can have a large impact in that spiritual development, but we do not desire to take the place of the family, and we very much want to reinforce and help you in that endeavor."

Each week middle school pastor Alan Mercer takes the time to write and send a newsletter to the parents of the youth in his ministry. This newsletter informs parents of current trends, keeps them up to date on what's happening in the ministry, and encourages them as they accept the primary role of helping their children grow in Christ.

their children to be equally important as the role played by the church or youth ministry.

- Ministries inviting students into a relationship with God through Jesus, baptizing them into the faith, and welcoming them on the journey to become like Jesus.

- Youth ministries prioritizing the development of followers of Jesus over the tactical engineering of mechanical ministries.

- Students seeing the importance of their "new" life today as much as their "eternal" life in the future.

I strongly believe that if we are to be relevant to the youth of today, our approach to ministry desperately needs reculturing. We need to incorporate new ideas and practices that flow out of deeply rooted biblical purposes. We need to make a new commitment to an ancient way. We need to do all we can to assure that we are making disciples who see themselves as agents of God's restoration and storytellers of a life-altering narrative. We need a new kind of youth ministry, a ministry that will help us more effectively make disciples in today's cultural context and honor God as we attentively foster growth in students.

1

RECULTURING EVANGELISM

From Carnivals and Bridges to Sharing the Journey

A few years ago, a well-known evangelist rolled into Minnesota's Twin Cities for a two-day evangelistic rally designed to reach teenagers for Christ. The event was a blend of concerts, extreme sports, junk food, t-shirt stands, and a series of gospel messages all in a carnival-like atmosphere.

I remember strolling with a colleague and friend through the capitol grounds in downtown St. Paul where the event was being held. We agreed that things looked rather positive. We saw thousands of people having a good time—interacting with one another, playing games, eating, and buying t-shirts with stupid sayings on them. There were lots of families hanging out together, which is always a cool thing to see. And there was a part of each of us that wished we had taken more of a leadership role in the planning and organization of the event, as we'd been invited to do nearly a year earlier.

But the other part of us was incredibly glad we hadn't taken a leadership role. It wasn't just that our joining the leadership team would have meant expending excessive amounts of time, energy, and effort to make the event happen—although that was certainly true. The primary reason we were glad we hadn't taken a larger role in this event was because that would have communicated to the rest of the leadership team and the wider evangelical church community that we considered event evangelism to be effective in revealing the kingdom of God. Nothing could be further from the truth.

As we continued to reflect after returning home from the event, my friend Tony and I realized that the part within each of us that wished we'd taken a leadership role on the task force was the self-seeking part. It was the part of us that covets the applause for big things getting accomplished. Do you ever do things for that reason?

It's not that I don't believe the event was good for the city. It was good because it brought short-term jobs to people and revenue to the local businesses. It was good because Christians poured into the downtown area where many of them confronted (perhaps for the first time) the thousands of homeless people living there. It was also good because hundreds of churched people were able to rally around a common ambition, and a sense of partnership was established among churches in the metro area. And it was also good because people heard about Jesus from a very good communicator and a snapshot of Jesus' story was told on local news stations. By and large, I think the event was good. But was it effective in its goal of making new disciples? I am not too sure about that.

I wonder how many of the counted "conversions" at this event were genuine. I wonder if all the time spent was worth it. I still speculate with friends about what other things might have been done with the thousands of dollars spent to pull the event off. So many of the students and parents I talked with thought the event was a great experience. They got a thrill seeing the best Christian skaters in the nation do their thing and hearing some mediocre Christian musicians act like superstars. But few of them invited any of their not-yet-believing friends, neighbors, coworkers, teammates, or relatives to join them.

All of which causes me to ask questions like: Should we put our efforts into event evangelism any longer? Do people who are not-yet believers even come to our events? Do Christians even invite not-yet believers to attend? Considering all the time, money, and effort spent on event evangelism, how much is really accomplished?

While driving through southern Georgia recently, I saw a series of billboards advertising a "Mega-Revival." The billboards stated a desire to see "thousands of youth from southern Georgia" united together to see the "magical illusions" of a magician I'd never heard of. (I'm sure he had a huge bag of tricks...) Of course, the billboards also featured another guy who appeared to be a preacher (chubby face, glasses, mustache, slicked-back hair, and sweat dripping down the side of his brow) who was going to share with these thousands of youth a "once and for all" story that could give them "life forever."

Most youth ministries in North America favor a more relational and personal method of evangelism over this mass revival style. Rightly so, I contend. We have learned that students in many of our contexts need a connection to the gospel being proclaimed—and that connection needs to be real and relational. For many ministries, that has meant primarily a combination of friendship evangelism and event evangelism.

This is a model I followed through much of my own ministry over the last decade. I've emphasized the importance of providing "strategic exposure" for the not-yet-believing students in our communities. The idea behind "strategic exposure" events is quite simple. We challenge students to bring *their* friends to an event that *we* plan, organize, and pay for. We always assure our students that the event will not humiliate or embarrass them in any way. Such events are usually built around a theme designed to attract and entertain students from all walks of life, such as themes built around sports, holidays, movies, or music.

We sought to plan events that would include: 1) an engaging activity (such as a movie, a competition, a race, or a horror house); 2) a talk that plants the gospel message in the minds and (hopefully) hearts of the youth; and 3) a chance to discuss that gospel message around some kind of food. In theory, this method of combining friendship evangelism and

THE MUSTARD SEED JAM HOUSE
Rob Thrasher
www.myspace.com/mustardseedjamhouse

The Mustard Seed Jam House is a coffeehouse ministry run by Downtown Ministries in Greenville, Pennsylvania, about two hours north of Pittsburgh. Rob Thrasher runs the coffeehouse ministry, which hosts concerts every Thursday and Saturday night, featuring a wide range of Christian bands. Rob's passion is to use music as the channel for connecting with the hurting, confused, seeking, and skeptical students of Greenville. Through conversation, coffee, and quality music, Rob and his volunteer team seek to encourage students to begin the journey with Jesus by developing lasting relationships characterized by the "hide-nothing, tell-everything, share-anything" mindset of life-dynamic evangelism.

event evangelism works. Students from all walks of life—jocks, gear-heads, nerds, greenies, and geeks are all welcome. And sometimes they come.

We normally consider these events a success if youth bring their not-yet-believing friends and their friends have a good time. If those visitors come back and participate in retreats and other church-based events then you are right on. Success!—especially if a few of the students "cross the line" from unbelief to belief along the way and become Christians, right? And even better if the senior pastor mentions those decisions during the service the following Sunday. That is the true measure of success, right?

Maybe. But after ten years of leading events like this, I'm not at all convinced that they are effective. I have witnessed thousands of students coming to events and just as many students who are excited to share their faith. These events were a doorway into the church for some young people who later decided to explore the faith and are now following Jesus. I don't doubt that at all. Most of those who have made a decision to follow Christ at our events became involved in our ministries in an ongoing way. So what's the problem? Well, there are several:

1) The students who graduate from our ministries know how to do evangelism only in the context of an event *we* have planned, organized, and paid for. We've never really modeled for them what it means to make disciples and invite and welcome people to follow Jesus.

2) Most of the students have relied on someone else to communicate the gospel. Even though we've raised up a few young emerging servants who are capable and passionate enough to share their connection story at an outreach event, we leave the majority of our students ill-equipped to share their faith.

3) This method of evangelism, the event/friendship combination, allows students to act in ways that are not at all Christ-

like outside these events, yet still feel they are honoring God by bringing friends to these events. Since students are obedient to that aspect of the Great Commission, they feel as though they are doing what a Christian is supposed to do. They never really face the challenge and discomfort of someone finding out how they really live with and love others.

4) Typically, youth ministries measure these events by the number of participants or the number of salvation prayers spoken. This unfortunate but common greed-producing fallacy pushes youth ministries to continually try to do more and more in order to get bigger and bigger. We end up living like "human doings" instead of human beings.

5) Students who have made a genuine commitment to submit their lives to Christ at these events are seldom followed up on and discipled. Most ministries just absorb the newbie into their existing discipleship-oriented programs and never offer specific help to the new Christian embarking on a journey of spiritual growth and discovery. We know the importance of discipling new believers, but let's be honest: True discipleship is not happening enough, is it?

6) In this model, we leaders are not held accountable for our own commitment to evangelism. In other words, students rarely if ever see evangelism modeled by their leaders. The planning and organizing of events can become the only "evangelism" we do.

7) The more events we plan and organize, the harder it is to break free from their gripping demands later down the road. And those pressing demands leave little space for reculturing—especially if your volunteer youth leaders, students, and the leadership of the church view the continual offering of more and more events as healthy. Most churches operate under the "if it ain't broke, don't fix it" mentality. This can make it extremely difficult to adjust to meet the spiritual needs of future generations.

I'm sure there are youth ministries in North America and elsewhere around the globe that are effectively reaching students for Christ using this combined event/friendship method of evangelism. But I tend to think the ministries that use this method effectively are few and far between.

BUILDING BRIDGES?

A lot of youth ministries killed event evangelism a long time ago and now focus entirely on a friendship evangelism method. And there's a lot to be said for this. It calls for Christian students to build bridges between themselves and their friends who are outside the church. This bridge is usually built on a common interest such as sports, academics, goals and dreams, family backgrounds, or employment. This bridge connects believing students with not-yet-believing students for the sole purpose of leading those not-yet-believing students to Christ. Friendship evangelism calls students to live like Jesus in the context of their relationships and care for their friends in a Good Samaritan kind of way.

I love bridges. My favorite bridge is a foot-and-bicycle bridge that Leonardo da Vinci designed 500 years ago. This bridge was recently built in Norway, after it had long been deemed impossible to build. One of the most beautiful sights I've ever seen was when I was on a plane taking off from the San Francisco airport early one morning and my eye caught the Golden Gate Bridge rising through the top of the morning fog. When I was attending college in New York, I used to stare at the Tappan Zee Bridge from my dorm room. There are a number of covered bridges across New England that my wife and I would stop the car and get out for. I love bridges.

I hate the analogy of bridge-building when we talk about evangelism, though. A bridge connects two places or points that are otherwise unable to connect. So what does it reveal when the church needs to build a bridge into the culture? It reveals a disconnection—a large separation between the culture and the church. On a more personal level it reveals a large separation between those who follow Christ and the not-yet-believing. But how long are the bridges we are building? How far are we from those in our lives who have not made a commitment to Christ?

A new kind of youth ministry is not about building bridges. It's not about constructing some artificial connection to others in a distant land. A new kind of youth ministry is committed to time and proximity. It means getting into the canoe and crossing the "waterways of life" together, in community, with your sphere of relations.

Obviously, there are many methods of evangelism. Some are effective for a season and then become irrelevant; others have been part of the fabric of the church for many years. You and your youth ministry may be using a method totally unlike the event or friendship methods. Maybe you are using the seeker small group method or the Sunday school method or the summer camp/retreat method. That's fine. It's up to you to decide what methods are best in your particular ministry context. As long as the gospel message of Jesus' life, death, and resurrection are being proclaimed and lived out effectively in your context, then do what you have to do. But if you aren't sure that your evangelism methods are effective, it may be time to reculture. It may be time for you to critically assess your current methods and incorporate new ideas and practices to see more students engage with Jesus.

EPIC MINISTRIES
Dan Schuster/Merlin Bartel
www.epicmx.com

Based in Calgary, Alberta, Epic Ministries seeks to mobilize the MX generations for Christ. Epic seeks to practice life-dynamic evangelism through house churches, worship experiences, and a downtown outreach center called The Urban Monastery. They have been known to host all-night prayer vigils at the Urban Monastery, as well as feeding the hungry and serving the homeless. They also encourage the people of their faith community to live missionally through the hosting/participation of their house churches, which are created to "gather with the expectation that the Holy Spirit will show up" and to "connect hearts and trust God to show us how to live in community."

THE HEART AND SOUL OF EVANGELISM

If we are going to effectively lead not-yet-believing students into a relationship with God through Jesus, I don't think it will be through the efforts of event evangelism or even friendship evangelism as we currently understand it. Instead, it will be through calling our students and leaders to a commitment of *life-dynamic evangelism.*

If you and I are going to join God in his global movement of transformation, we must do it through the moments of life that each of us experience and live. A life-dynamic approach to evangelism involves sharing the truths of God in the context of our everyday lives. It involves each of us connecting our heart and soul with the hearts and souls of those within our sphere of relations. It is faith sharing through the cycle of situations and circumstances we share with those in our world. It is an explanation of our faith both verbally and in our actions as the events of our lives unfold.

Life-dynamic faith sharing is authentic. It is a hide-nothing, tell-everything, and share-anything mindset that seeks to echo Christ's life and shine some light into the darkness of our world. Life-dynamic evangelism is not about *them* and *us.* It is not about *other* people or the people *out there.* Life-dynamic evangelism is about seeing people as *people.* Life-dynamic evangelism doesn't need bridges—just committed people who love God and others so much that their entire lives become missionally connected to God's plan to use us, the church, to join him in restoring the world.

Consider the following characteristics of life-dynamic evangelism:

1) Life-dynamic evangelism involves sharing our lived faith with those around us in the midst of the continuous change, activity, and progress of our lives.

2) It requires living in community with people who are not yet followers of Christ. This means being seen as Jesus-like, a friend of sinners.

3) It requires the wisdom, humility, and honesty to open our lives to others, including the elements of fear, doubt, and confusion that are part of our own journeys of faith.

4) It is faith sharing as Jesus did. It is about allowing others to join us in our journey, discover the truth, and then allowing them to come to their own decisions and understandings about following Christ.

5) It means allowing not-yet-believing people to speak into our lives and impart their own wisdom, knowledge, and skill. Are Christ-followers the only ones who can help you move through the trials of your life?

6) It is the faithful sharing of the story we find ourselves in *now*, not the story of our conversion *then*. Of course, the moment you accepted Christ is essential. But what is your story like now? Are you living a God-honoring life today? If so, invite others to share the journey with you. And if you are struggling, invite others to share that part of the journey with you. That's the point. It's about now. It's about authenticity—so let's take off our masks.

7) Life-dynamic evangelism is not just about a single occurrence like a special event or a friend-level act of service. It is about immersing ourselves in something way bigger than any of us—God's restorative plan.

8) It is not necessarily about a high volume of people. It is about the two or three people who are closest to you and do not yet know Christ—people for whom you can be Christ in a genuine way.

9) It does not come exclusively from a commitment to the Great Commission. It flows also out of a Great Commandment love of God and a love for people.

10) It is living your faith, not just talking about it.

In an age of certain change manifesting itself in uncertain ways, life-dynamic evangelism has great potential to reach the distrustfully curious and the faithfully skeptical. I believe it is essential for youth pastors to begin developing and implementing a ministry culture that allows students to better understand how they might be Jesus to their family, friends, and the wider community.

I can't offer you a step-by-step plan to follow in reculturing your own evangelism ministry. As the chief architect of your ministry, you are the one who best knows what suits your own context. But in seeking to foster a new kind of evangelism, you'll want to focus on equipping students so they can use both major and trivial events in their lives as opportunities to engage with the people around them. This means continuing to train students theologically—but with an emphasis on practicing their faith, rather than simply believing all the right things. Emphasis would also be placed on developing practical relationship-building skills such as listening, sharing, caring, and communicating for the purpose of deepening the sense of community.

Your recultured evangelism would be driven by the goal of connecting students with God through Jesus, not packing a calendar full of events for the purpose of appearing active. Youth events would be understood primarily as gatherings where life-dynamic evangelism can take place, rather than the events themselves serving as the evangelism method.

Rethinking our evangelism approach also means providing space for students who are still exploring their faith to participate in certain roles that have too long been reserved "for believers only." These might include participating on the worship team, attending discipleship-oriented retreats, and traveling with mission teams. In this "play before you pay" era, students must be given the chance to belong before they believe.

Ministries oriented around life-dynamic evangelism require paid and volunteer leaders who model this method of evangelism on a regular basis. Students can't just see the adults leading their ministries as event organizers. They must also see us as people who live in ways that reveal the kingdom of God to all those around us.

Our evangelism design will require constant reculturing to remain relevant and accessible. We must be speaking the language of an emerging culture, and those immersed in that culture must perceive our ministries as near to their heart. We must dare to reculture in the midst of the tensions surrounding programming, tradition, and skepticism. But if we are going to make an impact in our world, moving in the direction of life-dynamic evangelism is not just an option, but a necessity.

After over a decade of planning and executing outreach events, I can honestly say we've seen more students come to Jesus through relationships and one-on-one life sharing than through any entertaining event or flashy program. Such events may wow your students for a while, but it's the hard work of relational evangelism and sharing in God's mission to restore the world that brings about God's desired outcome of missional living—people proclaiming and living out God's epic story.

FOR REFLECTION AND DISCUSSION:

- What method of evangelism do you and your team use currently? Is it working? Are students meeting Jesus and choosing to follow him? Are you welcoming new believers into your ministry?

- How well is your ministry equipping students to share and show Jesus? What can you do better?

- How can you teach life-dynamic evangelism and structure your ministry to better encourage it?

- Are you and your other adult leaders modeling life-dynamic evangelism?

2 RECULTURING DISCIPLESHIP

From Learning *about* God to Living *for* God

I am not sure when I first started to question the way I was discipling youth. Maybe it was when A.J., one of the guys in my group, commented, "I come here every week, and I have a good time. I listen to you, and sometimes even go home and look up the Web sites you talk about. But sometimes I just don't get how any of this information helps me be a different person." Or maybe it was the night when another student, Leigh, came to me after I'd spent the evening teaching and said, "So what does any of this have to do with my future?"

For nearly ten years I saw discipleship training as filling students with as much theological information as I could before they graduated high school—in hopes that they would not also "graduate Jesus" when they completed school. All of our discipleship programs were very similar. The events were all designed for me or another adult to present truths from God's word.

You might say, "What's wrong with that?" Well, I'll tell you what's wrong with it. Students' lives don't change just from learning more and more information—even if that information is all true and all about God. We may be the greatest communicators on the planet—creative, charismatic, clear, compelling, comical—but that doesn't guarantee our students are connecting with what it really means to be a developing follower of Jesus. Discipleship is not solely about learning more about God. It's about learning how to live one's life to glorify God. A new kind of youth ministry understands the importance of spiritual formation in youth ministry and becomes more intentional about nurturing spiritual growth in students.

The term *spiritual formation* gets thrown around a lot in churches these days. The term has become a buzzword for youth workers—a trendy way of signifying our relevance to a younger generation of Christ-followers. I've noticed that talking about spiritual formation is often used as "proof" that we are aware of the advances of the emerging church and are associating ourselves with those advances. I recently asked a youth worker from western

Canada, "So what is it about spiritual formation that intrigues you?" She responded, "I don't really know. I guess it's just the postmodern, emergent way of doing church."

I love the way the emerging church movement is helping the church rethink its purpose and methods. But spiritual formation is not an idea born out of Brian McLaren's books. It is not a new concept—it is an ancient one. I'm not suggesting that the emerging church advance has claimed ownership of the phrase. But I do think most youth workers both know and like the fact that frequent use of the phrase *spiritual formation* can both raise parents' eyebrows and get them an immediate appointment on their senior pastor's calendar. Nonetheless, I think that spiritual formation is an essential concept for youth workers to understand—and to help others understand.

Consider these words of author Dallas Willard in a 2005 article from *Christianity Today:*

> Spiritual formation in a Christian tradition answers a specific human question: *What kind of person am I going to be?* It is the process of establishing the character of Christ in the person. That's all it is. You are taking on the character of Christ in a process of discipleship to him under the direction of the Holy Spirit and the Word of God. It isn't anything new, because Christians have been in this business forever. They haven't always called it *spiritual formation*, but the term itself goes way back.

Willard's words about spiritual formation speak to the heart of our task of encouraging discipleship. Our goal is not just to transfer information about God to our students. Our goal is to equip our students to answer Willard's question: "What kind of person am I going to be?"

MOVING STUDENTS FROM A STATIC FAITH TO A MOBILE FAITH

When our discipleship design is built around relaying information about God to students rather than nurturing their spiritual growth, it can lead to a *static* faith. A static faith cannot move; it may appear to be authentic or sincere, but it offers little opportunity for growth, change, or progression. But when formation is the chief ingredient of our discipleship design, we encourage students toward a *mobile* faith—a faith they can take with them for the rest of their journey.

Let me be clear: I think both information and formation are needed for a developing follower of Jesus to mature and truly develop. Yet emphasis solely on information transfer leads students to a static faith. Like someone who lies so much they begin to believe their own lies, students may think that by learning about God they've developed a faith that is genuine and growing. They may be quite sincere about this. Sadly, these students do not realize that unless their faith is demonstrated through inward and outward formation, that faith is underdeveloped and often left idle.

A new kind of youth ministry seeks to help students develop a faith that is mobile—a faith they can take with them along the way, wherever that way leads them. Reculturing our discipleship efforts to focus more deeply on the inward and outward formation of our students is imperative to the growth of each individual follower and the entire church community.

In my own ministry as well as my observations of others, I've seen too many students who graduate our ministries without really knowing what it means to follow Jesus. Sadly, many students leave with one of two false perspectives about the Christian faith.

On the one hand, some students leave our ministries thinking the Christian faith is just a set of rules, legalistic behaviors, rigid beliefs, and complex stories—all for the purpose of making faith a difficult "thing" to commit to. Given this understanding, it's not surprising that many of these students depart our ministries feeling that such a bulky and unbending faith will be of little help to them on the next stage of their journeys. Such youth decide their lives need not be obstructed by a faith that asks so much of them.

Other students leave our ministries thinking faith is hardly worth their time. While they may similarly see faith as full of legalistic rules and rigidity, their problem is not that faith is too difficult to give their lives to, but that it doesn't seem worth giving their lives to. They can't see how the faith they've been taught really offers them help in the "real world," so they leave our ministries deciding not to take their faith with them at all. I have seen far too many students make a calculated decision to leave Jesus and all they have come to know about God behind. I contend that they do this because we've not given an understanding of how to practice their faith in an everyday context. Their faith is not a mobile faith.

ECHO

Mike Novelli/Caesar Kalinowski
www.echothestory.com

Echo provides consultation, training, and online resources to help youth and adults actively engage with the Scripture through a process known as "Chronological Bible Storying" (or "Storying"). Through the telling of Bible stories in sequential order and a related process of dialogue and discovery, Echo seeks to help people realize a new and deeper connection with God's redemptive plan and the truths found in the Bible. Echo hopes to help people see themselves differently in light of the "redemptive arc" of God's story, thereby encouraging deeper and more meaningful worship, building biblical community, and nurturing the emergence of a community of storytellers!

If we want our students to carry their faith with them after high school graduation, we have to help them see how that faith makes a difference. It's imperative that we give our students more than just a bunch of stories *about* God. We need to help our students understand the story of God—and their own role in God's story.

THE STORY OF GOD

It wasn't until a few years ago that I really began thinking about the story of God. I mean, I spent my entire life learning Bible stories, many of which were entertaining, fun, and—depending on how they were taught—sometimes helpful to my spiritual nourishment. But it wasn't until sometime after I'd completed a Bible college degree and a graduate degree in theological studies that the story of

God finally clicked with me. It was only then that I realized the real story is how God is restoring the world and how he is using people like me to do it. That's the story of God that underlies all the stories in Scripture. But for some reason I never got the big picture of what God is doing, and no one ever really helped connect the dots for me.

I went through a childhood of Bible stories and then years of theological training as an adult before I realized God is in the process of restoring the world. That is to say that he is bringing it back to its original condition—perfect. God is in the process of bringing his relationship with humanity back to its original condition and intent. When we trace God's story throughout the Bible, we see this beautiful and wonderful restoration process unfold.

One helpful way of discovering and interacting with the story of God is to view it in episodes. Each episode is an important event in itself, but also a distinct part of a greater whole. Viewing God's story in seven episodes can help us see "the big picture," allowing us to more deeply take hold of God's constant pursuit to restore humanity unto himself.

EPISODE	KEY VERSE	BIG IDEA
CREATION	In the beginning God created the heavens and the earth. Now the earth was formless and empty, darkness was over the surface of the deep, and the Spirit of God was hovering over the waters. (Genesis 1:1-2)	God's creative act serves as the origin of our world and our story. The story begins with God and his desire to create our world.
THE FALL	When the woman saw that the fruit of the tree was good for food and pleasing to the eye, and also desirable for gaining wisdom, she took some and ate it. She also gave some to her husband, who was with her, and he ate it. Then the eyes of both of them were opened, and they realized they were naked; so they sewed fig leaves together and made coverings for themselves. (Genesis 3:6-7)	The crisis. Not long into the story, sin impacts and infects God's entire created world. No one can escape the stain of sin.

A NEW KIND OF YOUTH MINISTRY

EPISODE	KEY VERSE	BIG IDEA
PROMISE OF RESTORATION	The Lord had said to Abram, "Leave your country, your people and your father's household and go to the land I will show you. I will make you into a great nation and I will bless you; I will make your name great, and you will be a blessing. I will bless those who bless you, and whoever curses you I will curse; and all peoples on earth will be blessed through you." (Genesis 12:1-3)	God makes a promise to restore the created order through a relationship with Abraham and his descendents.
PEOPLE OF GOD	When the Lord saw that he [Moses] had gone over to look [at the burning bush], God called to him from within the bush, "Moses! Moses!" And Moses said, "Here I am." (Exodus 3:4) And the Lord has declared this day that you are his people, his treasured possession as he promised, and that you are to keep all his commands. (Deuteronomy 26:18)	God begins fulfilling his promise to restore the world by providing land, laws, and leaders to a nation who will be known to the world as the people of God. For some 1500 years, the people of Israel struggle to remain faithful to God.
JESUS	While they were there, the time came for the baby to be born, and she gave birth to her firstborn, a son. (Luke 2:6-7) It was now about the sixth hour, and darkness came over the whole land until the ninth hour, for the sun stopped shining. And the curtain of the temple was torn in two. Jesus called out with a loud voice, "Father, into your hands I commit my spirit." When he had said this, he breathed his last. (Luke 23:44-46) Why do you look for the living among the dead? He is not here; he has risen! (Luke 24:5-6)	Jesus, God's Son, comes to earth and through his life, death, and resurrection, fulfills his Father's promise of restoration. Now, through faith in Jesus, the powers of sin and death have been defeated, and a relationship with God is available to all who receive him.

EPISODE	KEY VERSE	BIG IDEA
THE DISCIPLES & THE CHURCH	Then Jesus said to Simon, "Don't be afraid; from now on you will catch men." So they pulled their boats up on shore, left everything and followed him. (Luke 5:10-11) Then Jesus came to them and said, "All authority in heaven and on earth has been given to me. Therefore, go and make disciples of all nations, baptizing them in the name of the Father and of the Son and of the Holy Spirit, and teaching them to obey everything I have commanded you. And surely I am with you always, to the very end of the age. (Matthew 28:18-20) Those who accepted his message were baptized…They devoted themselves to the apostles' teaching and to the fellowship, to the breaking of bread and to prayer. Everyone was filled with awe… (Acts 2:41-43)	Jesus calls the church community to live out the story and lead others, through love, to join in God's mission of restoring the world.
A WORLD RESTORED	Then I saw a new heaven and a new earth, for the first heaven and the first earth had passed away, and there was no longer any sea…And I heard a loud voice from the throne saying, "Now the dwelling of God is with men, and he will live with them. They will be his people, and God himself will be with them and be their God. (Revelation 21:1,3)	At the end of all things, all starts anew as God completely restores his creation and dwells with his people forever!

If students get beyond our youth ministries without realizing how God's mission is at work all around us, and how God is using us to accomplish that mission, I fear they will never feel led to give their whole selves to God. When students leave our ministries without an ability to put the Bible stories, memory verses, and theological concepts into a larger biblical framework that makes sense, they depart our ministries without a mobile faith. As spiritual directors, we must help students embrace the entire narrative of God and see their role in the story. We must also help them develop holy instincts that will form sacred rhythms, behaviors, and practices in their lives.

Helping students see the restorative nature of God and their own role as agents of restoration not only gives the students a context but also invites a life-long commitment. And this commitment is the very thing that will secure their faith when they go off to college or hit the "real world". Too often our students' faith sways when they leave our ministries because they've been connected to a passionate leader or a relevant community, but not committed to a mission—the mission of God. Those other things are great—but not when they take the place of or overshadow a commitment to the mission of God.

As the "God-With-Us" episode of the chart above illustrates, Jesus was used by God, as God, to initiate the calling of agents of restoration for generations to come. Through his life, death, and resurrection, Jesus defeats the power of sin and death and fulfills his Father's promise of restoration. Through faith in Jesus, a relationship with God is open to all. That is the heart of the gospel message.

But just as Jesus was used by God, God also wants to use each of us. As individual disciples and as a body or community responsible to make disciples (Matthew 28:19-20), we join Jesus as participants or agents of restoration. God is using you and me and the rest of the church throughout the world to help reestablish the original, perfect relationship between God and his people.

Students need to know this. They need to understand the integral part that they play in the mission of God. I fear that most students who travel with us throughout their teenage years end up missing the most important aspect of their own restoration—that they can be used of God to restore others! That is, students need to know that the way they declare their faith through actions and words is an opportunity to restore people through the power of the gospel.

Most ministries teach youth the Great Commission—challenging them to share their faith with their peers, sit with the students at lunch who are sitting alone, and invite their teammates to outreach events. But God invites us all to something bigger. God invites us to recognize that the story of God is unfolding around us each day, and that we share in God's mission by becoming agents of restoration. Recognizing our calling to fulfill the Great Commission is one thing. But recognizing that in doing so we become partners with God in his mission of restoring the world is so much more.

KEY VIRTUES OF JESUS

Another big reason why students are not able to move past a static faith and form a faith that is mobile is because we youth workers talk more with our students about what they should not do as Christians rather than encouraging them in what they should do. We talk a lot about not sinning, but sometimes we do very little to help students form faith habits that will nurture them as disciples— habits that help them celebrate in their jubilant moments and fight through the times of struggle, temptation, and confusion.

Scot McKnight, author of *The Jesus Creed* and many other valuable works, defines a disciple as one who "engages with Jesus as a person by trusting him and, because of that relationship, begins to *live out the virtues* Jesus talks about." McKnight's definition pulls me in for several reasons. First, it makes mention of Jesus as the person in whom we trust. We trust or believe in the Truth—Jesus. Second, I like the way the word *relationship* speaks to what it means to "engage with Jesus." I think the idea of faith as a "relationship" with Jesus might be a tenet of our orthodoxy that we need to spend more time helping students comprehend. A relationship is built on trust. You love someone you trust. Therefore, if you do not trust, you do not love. Third, I appreciate that

McKnight's definition of disciple involves an action-oriented response. Discipleship isn't about just being a learner or a student of theological reflection. It's about living out your trust in Jesus in relationship with him. Finally, I like the definition because it speaks to the virtues of Jesus' life—the particular qualities and characteristics that make Jesus worth following.

What then are these virtues of Jesus we need to help our students live out so their faith might be mobile? Well, the gospels are full of them, and they are all significant. Personally, I'd contend that we can help students live in the way of Jesus by considering the virtues he demonstrated through his (1) *surrendering* to God, (2) *abiding* in God, and (3) *reflecting* the nature of God.

To surrender is to give over or resign. Jesus was a surrendered person. He denied himself and gave his will over to the Father (John 6:38; Matthew 6). Jesus' goal was to be used by his Father so he might be the one through whom restoration is accessible.

To abide with someone is to journey or dwell with that person. Jesus abided with the Father. He understood the importance of spending time with God. Throughout the gospels we see Jesus withdrawing from the business and crowds surrounding him to spend time alone with his Father in prayer (John 14:20, Luke 5:16, Mark 1:35).

To reflect is to show or mirror the image and characteristics of another. Jesus persistently

YOUTHFRONT

Mike King
www.youthfrontzone.com

YouthFront is a ministry based in Shawnee, Kansas, which seeks to bring young people into a growing relationship with Jesus Christ through a variety of ministry programs including summer camps, mission endeavors, campus ministry, and worship experiences. One of their camps, YouthFront Camp South, was designed as a haven for students along their spiritual journey—a place to rest in God's creation, gaze upon its beauty, and grow in your relationship with Him.

The genius of YouthFront Camp South is that it balances times of solitude and worship with interactive sports activities like swimming, hiking, and high-ropes. Students who attend camp get more than just fun and games and a Bible lesson every now and then--they get times of directed silence and spiritual guidance. Rather than seeing themselves as program directors who plan activities while trying to help young people avoid broken legs and stay out of mischief, counselors see themselves primarily as spiritual directors who help youth deepen their faith.

displayed the attributes of God, thereby revealing the very nature of God. The hope, grace, compassion, love, justice, and righteousness we see in Jesus throughout the gospels are reflections of God's very person and character.

Young people need to know that Jesus invites us to join him on this continuing journey of learning to surrender to God, abide in God, and reflect God's nature. His invitation to us is the same as the one he offered his first disciples in Mark 1:14-18:

> After John was put in prison, Jesus went into Galilee, proclaiming the good news of God. "The time has come!" he said. "The Kingdom of God is near! Repent and believe the Good News!"
>
> As Jesus walked beside the Sea of Galilee, he saw Simon and his brother Andrew casting a net into the lake, for they were fisherman. "Come, follow me," Jesus said, "and I will make you fishers of men." At once they left their nets and followed him.

I contend that in calling people to *repent, believe,* and *follow* him, Jesus was not inviting them solely to salvation. I believe it was also a call toward holiness, a call to imitate him. Jesus' words are also an invitation to enter into a perpetual cycle of soul change that increases both the frequency and duration of the holy moments in our lives. Jesus' words repent, believe and follow are the elements of an ongoing journey I refer to as the "cycle of spiritual transformation." When students understand faith as being about surrendering to God, abiding in Jesus, and learning to imitate Jesus in all they are and all they are becoming, their faith will be active and alive.

HELPING STUDENTS EXPERIENCE THE CYCLE OF SPIRITUAL TRANSFORMATION

Kenda Dean is professor of youth, church and culture at Princeton Theological Seminary and author of such brilliant works as *Practic-*

ing Passion and *The Godbearing Life.* I recently wrote and asked Dean what we can do to help give our youth a mobile faith. That is, what do students need from their churches and youth ministries to help them continue to practice their faith after they "leave" our ministries? She responded:

> If young people are to practice faith when they "graduate" from youth ministry, the most important gift churches can give them is lifestyle faith instead of program faith. Of course, that doesn't mean that Christian programs don't have a role to play. But young people aren't looking for programs; and when the church makes faith into "one more thing to do," we turn the gospel into an extracurricular activity, one among dozens, and in so doing we gut it of its transforming significance. The last thing postmodern young people need is something more to do. They have plenty to keep them busy, but precious little to make them holy. The only portable faith is a lifestyle faith, a *habitus*, a way of life, a rule to live out in a community that "kneads the dough" of the soul, and through these practices opens young people up to what God is already doing in them and in the world.

I couldn't agree more. You and I must help each other discover the best ways to help students develop a way of living that "kneads the dough" of the soul. Our efforts to encourage discipleship cannot be just presentations of important information for the mind. Encouraging discipleship in a new kind of youth ministry must be focused on formation of the whole person—the heart, mind, soul, and strength.

But how do we balance the important goal of teaching the Scriptures and theology with the need to teach practices that nourish the soul such as prayer, meditation, simplicity, fasting, and confession? In other words, how do we balance information and formation?

Again, I find Kenda Dean's words helpful:

> Orthodoxy—or "faithful thinking"—has long been the foothold of theological education. But orthopraxy—or the faithful practice of Christian life—has been the way the church has formed disciples for centuries. Discipleship isn't something you learn just by studying it; at some point you have to do it. Arguing whether information or experiences of formation come first is a chicken and egg argument; it really doesn't matter, since both are essential to Christian discipleship. Spiritual disciplines, or practices, are simply enacted beliefs; they're embodied orthodoxy. Theological study is simply the unpacking of centuries of Christian life that gave rise to texts and traditions along the way. Orthodoxy and orthopraxy—faithful belief and faithful practice—are the two lungs of Christian discipleship. You can get along breathing on only one lung, but you can't breathe very deeply, and you don't live as long or as fully as when you use both lungs, which is clearly what God intends.

POSITIONAL AND PRACTICAL SANCTIFICATION: TWO ASPECTS OF BECOMING HOLY

Dr. Floyd Barackman, my theology professor at Davis College in New York, was the first to really call me to focus on inward formation. He was always telling me the Christian faith is not just about your eternal life, it's about your new life today and what you're doing with it. In conversations over coffee or tea in the college cafeteria, he would remind me that by faith in Christ I have already been *positionally* set apart by God. But *practically* I need to be working to continue to purge myself of all things that are not of God and that keep me from coming nearer to God.

In his book, *Practical Christian Theology* (Kregel Publications, 2001), Barackman discusses how these two different aspects of sanctification function to bring us closer to God. Positionally, Barackman says, it is our *standing* through faith in Jesus that brings us near to God (1 Corinthians 1:2,30; 6:11). But practically, it is the *condition* of our daily lives that brings us closer to God, or separates us from God and his will.

Consider this comparison of positional and practical sanctification:

POSITIONAL SANCTIFICATION	PRACTICAL SANCTIFICATION
It relates to our standing in Christ.	It relates to our condition of daily life.
It occurs over the process of salvation.	It occurs throughout our lifetime.
It is God's instantaneous work.	It is God's progressive work.
It is complete and absolute.	It is incomplete and relative.
It is the same for every believer.	It is varies with each believer.
It makes each believer a saint.	It makes each believer saintly.

Now, before you jump to any conclusions about me, understand that I'm aware of the debates surrounding the theological positions derived from the illustration above. Whether you believe that God's work of salvation occurs instantaneously or that our salvation occurs as God works progressively over the course of our lives isn't really the point—at least it isn't *my* point.

My point is to build momentum for a new kind of youth ministry that can help students realize the new life they have in Jesus. When we are aware of these two different aspects of sanctification, we are better able to encourage students toward lives that follow the way of Jesus. If we can help our youth see the importance of continually purging themselves from sin and living out the new life we've been given (Romans 6:4), then we are on our way to helping them increase the frequency and duration of the holy moments in their lives.

A new kind of youth ministry is intentional about forming students spiritually. Leaders in this new kind of youth ministry consider themselves spiritual directors, not program directors. Rather than focusing on innovation and invention to better transfer information to students, they are preoccupied with creating and sustaining a formative approach to developing followers of Jesus.

A reculturing must occur within the core of youth ministry. We must stop pretending that our events, activities, and programs suffice for the spiritual development of students. While events, activities and programs can open doors for our assisting in the spiritual development of students, they can never be the primary tool for developing followers of Jesus who live, love, and lead in his way.

FOR REFLECTION AND DISCUSSION:

- How do you define discipleship?

- What is spiritual formation?

- Do your students understand God's overarching storyline?

- Do they realize their role in God's mission?

- How can you better help your students embody the virtues of Jesus?

- Do your students understand the cycle of spiritual transformation that is represented in the words *repent*, *believe*, and *follow*?

- What is sanctification? In what ways are both positional and practical sanctification critical parts of the Christian life? Do your students understand this?

3 RECULTURING SERVICE AND OUTREACH

From Meeting Others' Needs to Living amidst Their Need

As I sat there in the living room with a few adult leaders and our student ministry team planning our next outreach event, I found myself a bit uncomfortable. At first, I wasn't sure why. I knew I was doing a good thing in helping our student leaders plan and organize as well as in calling them to make a commitment. With a bit of a knot in my stomach I looked around at "the cream of the crop" I had so carefully selected and assembled and asked myself, "What am I doing? Is youth ministry really about getting students to buy into my vision and then giving them the basic 'skills' for a life of peer ministry? Is this how Jesus equipped His followers? Is youth ministry about just imparting skills or imparting your life and inspiring to a new way of life?"

I could feel the butterflies flying around my stomach. My palms were sweating and my ears were getting red. (That actually happens when I get self-conscious!) The students had no idea what I was wrestling with that night. They were continuing to prepare and plan, even as I was coming face-to-face with the knowledge that I wasn't doing enough to equip them for ministry. I was going to have to make a radical decision to dismantle this team and my plans in order to truly reculture the way I was equipping students.

My thoughts were interrupted when one student asked, "So, Pastor Chris, how many people do you think will come this year? Should we print more tickets than last year?" Another student followed up by asking, "Who is sharing the Gospel this year? Do you think any of us are ready?" The knot in my stomach grew larger as I realized that I'd created a team of 20-plus student ministry leaders who really had no idea what it meant to help their friends engage with Jesus. Declaring their faith to their friends had been reduced to wondering how many tickets we'd have to print and which student was "ready" to share the gospel.

We finished our meeting, and I waited until the last student was picked up by her parents (over 30 minutes late, of course). Feeling a bit numb, I climbed in my car and slowly drove home—all the while thinking about what it means to equip students. I was so engrossed in my thoughts that at one point I had to be reminded by the car's horn behind me that the light was green.

A few days later I left town for a personal retreat I'd been planning for some time. I'd been intending just to pray, sleep, and read, but God had other ideas in mind. I ended up spending the two days praying, yes, but also thinking around the idea of equipping students. I came away from that retreat with a new and valuable understanding. Up until that point in my ministry, I'd focused on developing in my students the elemental skills to *meet* the physical, spiritual, emotional and intellectual needs of their friends. I had not, however, been equipping and inspiring my students to *live* in the center of their friends' needs. The difference might not seem vast to you—but for me, it was a gigantic shift.

For over a decade I had been imparting basic skills to allow my students to minister to their peers. In actuality, I was usually just giving them knowledge for their heads and tasks for their hands. In most cases, their hearts were going untouched and uninspired.

Meeting the physical, spiritual, emotional, and intellectual needs of our friends is extremely important. I do not want to minimize the efforts of anyone who is passionately committed to doing so. I contend, however, that when we equip students solely to *meet* needs, we have missed the point. The point isn't to meet needs here and there as we have opportunity or when we feel like it. The point isn't to serve others when it's convenient for us. The point is to determinedly live in the middle of others' needs—that is, to develop a lifestyle of caring for and serving others.

MORE THAN APOLOGETICS

Before we talk any more about living amidst others' needs, it's important to be sure we're on the same page. When I speak of equipping students to meet needs, I am not referring primarily to training students in apologetics. I'm not talking about training youth to defend their faith.

I believe that apologetics, the branch of theology concerned with providing the truths of Christianity, is very important to our faith (1 Peter 3:15). But I don't think it is what many youth workers in recent decades have made it—the number one thing we equip our students with. We make a big mistake when we jump past helping students know what it means to love others in an effort to give them skills to defend their faith. While I wholeheartedly believe we need to help students develop the ability to articulate what they believe, I am strongly against equipping them with "skills to defend"—as if the conversations they have with their friends are some sort of game or, even worse, some battle they must win.

There are two primary reasons why I think it's a mistake to overemphasize defending the faith as we train our students. First, I'm not sure many students are in a culture where they have to "defend" what they believe. Most students are "allowed" to believe whatever they wish. For the most part, their friends are probably pluralists who don't care what they believe or even if they do believe. Most students aren't in a position where they must defend their faith as much as they have opportunities to articulate their faith. (Incidentally, I contend that an accurate interpretation of 1 Peter 3:15 would urge us to be "prepared to articulate" what we believe as opposed to being "prepared to wage war and defend" what we believe.)

Second, I'm not sure most middle school or high school students are mature enough emotionally to handle a conversation in which a "defense" of the faith is required. I have witnessed over the years that the passion of students and the need to be "right" can make it difficult for them to engage in a meaningful conversation in which they must articulate what they believe.

A new kind of youth ministry calls students beyond just verbal exchange of the truths of Christianity and helps them develop lifestyles that communicate the truths of Christianity. Apologetics is not merely about concrete facts, logic, and reason. It is about embracing the mysteries of God and life, and through those mysteries discovering what it means to reveal the illogical and unreasonable truths of Christianity. It is not about winning arguments about issues like creationism and the end times—and all the historical claims that come between them. Rather, it is about getting to the place in our lives where we can proclaim the truth of our faith by the way we love God and love others.

I am all for helping students know how to articulate their faith in order to help others better understand why Christians believe what they do. But I believe we can serve the church better when we equip students with a mindset in which they seek to serve others first and articulate the faith later. It seems simple—but don't the best conversations about faith come out of time spent with others, building trust with them, serving them, and loving them? The best conversations I've had about faith with friends who are not- yet believers flow out of relationships in which life is shared, not dis-agreements about our theological understandings.

MEETING NEEDS OR LIVING AMIDST THEM?

So how do we make the shift from a simple focus on training students to meet needs to equipping students to live amidst needs? How do we help youth embrace a new way of living, rather than simply looking for opportunities to help? I think there are at least five key principles that can help us do this reculturing.

Principle 1: There's no such thing as "us" and "them." It's all one big "us."

If students are really going to live amidst the needs of others, we need to help them stop drawing hard lines that divide the world into believers and unbelievers, Christians and non-Christians, us and them. Students must be encouraged to realize there is only one difference between who they are in Jesus and who their not-yet-believing friends are not in Jesus—grace. The only thing (granted, it is a *big* thing) that makes a believer distinctively different is the grace of God. When we remember that grace is all that separates those who believe and those who do not yet believe, it instills not only a great amount of gratitude to God for what he has done in our lives but also an awareness of the oneness of humanity. It's not anything we've done to create the difference between believer and not-yet believer; it's all God and God's grace.

Some followers of Jesus seem to believe that, at their very core, they are in some way better than those who do not follow Jesus—and that is not true. We believers have been pulled from the muck of sin and, therefore, are called into constant pursuit of holy lives. We know we didn't escape the muck on our own, of course. So why do many of us walk about our journey with an attitude of superiority and royalty? True, we are God's children—but so too are those who do not yet believe.

"Us and them" may be an accurate description of how we will be separated in times to come—heaven and hell. But that final judgment is up to God. For humanity to be separated now is ridiculous. Sanctification—or God's righteous act of setting us apart—is not about separating us from other people, it is about separating us from sin. We do not walk this earth as lost and saved, we walk this earth as humanity. We are one large and diverse group, all created by the same God. By God's grace, some of us are separated from our iniquity and will forever live in God's presence.

FELLOWSHIP BIBLE CHURCH

Chris Campbell
www.fbcbridgeport.org

Chris Campbell leads a vibrant youth ministry at the Fellowship Bible Church in Bridgeport, West Virginia, a culturally diverse area in which the rich and the poor are separated by a highway that runs through the middle of town. When I met Chris a few months ago while speaking at a conference, I was immediately struck by his passion to see the students in the local schools around his church discover a relationship with God. One of his efforts involved a revisioning of "See You at the Pole Day," a growing movement in which Christian youth gather before school on a particular day to pray together. Rather than encouraging his students simply to gather around the flagpole to pray for one another, he challenged them to gather the prayer needs of the entire school community. In preparation for the SYATP Day, the students in his ministry collected prayer needs from fellow students, faculty, coaches, and members of the administration and school board for nearly two weeks. When SYATP Day came, all those who had been asked to share prayer requests knew exactly why this group of Christians would be gathering around the pole—to pray for them! Chris and his students modeled what it means to enter into lives and live among the needs of others.

Drawing lines now is not helpful in our attempts to be agents of restoration. God is restoring the world, and many of us have been called out to help him do that. It doesn't make us special, just blessed. Students need to realize this. Frankly, the attitudes within some churches often do more harm than good.

My family and I attend a great church called The Well. The Well calls itself "a church without walls"—and that understanding is at the very core of its ministry. I love that my children are being mentored by folks who see humanity not as divided into "us" and "them" but as one large and diverse group of people. I love that the ones helping me nurture my children spiritually see the world not as good and evil but as good and God's. Is there evil in the world? Pick up the newspaper or jump on the Internet. Yes, there is evil—and some of it is even caused by believers who make bad choices.

I am not suggesting a pluralistic or relativistic attitude here. I know this world is comprised of those who believe and those who do not believe. I am, however, suggesting that if we want our students to seek to *live* among needs rather than merely *meet* needs, we must help them see humanity as one gathering of people, all created and loved by God. As agents of restoration, God invites us to cultivate authentic relationships with all people, share the gospel story of grace and freedom, and live alongside one another bringing justice and dignity to all.

Principle 2: "Should I help?" is the wrong question.

A couple of weeks ago I was leaving the office for a two-day road trip along with my good friend Mike Novelli, the associate director at Sonlife. Prepared for meetings as soon as we arrived, Mike and I were casually but very nicely dressed. Not long after leaving our offices, we noticed a woman and her children by the side of the road. She had driven her car off the road and into the snowy ditch. We could tell no one was injured because of her pace as she viewed her situation. As we slowly drove by, I said to Mike, "Should we stop and help her?" As soon as I said it, I knew it was the stupidest question I could possibly ask in this situation. The question shouldn't be, "Should we help her?" The question should be, "How can we help?"

Mike and I managed to rock her car back and forth enough so she could get some traction, and she was able to back out and be on her way. Midway through the endeavor, the woman asked us, "Are you sure you want to help? You are getting really wet and muddy."

"Yeah, no problem," we said. We resumed our drive from Chicago to South Bend, Indiana, covered in mud from head to toe.

If we are going to reculture the way we equip students for a life of ministry, it is important to get them asking the right questions. We need to help students move beyond asking "Should I help" to the more productive question, "How can I help?" Regardless of the situation, whether it be a driver in need on the side of the road or a street person in need of a hot meal and shower, we should not get slowed by trying to answer the wrong question.

We sometimes operate as if our students will never know how to serve appropriately unless we model it. So we take them to nursing homes, rescue missions, shelters, and other areas of need so they can serve and meet the needs of others. We do this because we want to help our students move beyond themselves and realize the world wasn't created for them; instead, they were created for the world. This is a very good and helpful mechanism for equipping that we should never stop pursuing.

But if we are really going to move students from asking "Should I help?" to asking "How can I help?" we need to help them do three things: develop a Kingdom perspective, be a humble presence in the lives of others, and reveal truth through justice and life-dynamic evangelization.

Developing a Kingdom Perspective: Essentially, a kingdom perspective is a "life is bigger than me" frame of mind. It is revealed in a life that demonstrates greater concern for others than for ourselves. A kingdom perspective is rooted in the understanding and desire to help God accomplish his mission of restoring the world rather than being about one's own personal mission. Through serving others, students gain greater compassion, embrace a life beyond their own, and become more alert and responsive to the needs of others. In short, they begin to see people through the eyes of Jesus.

Being a Humble Presence: Being a humble presence means having a compassionate manner. It means interacting with people in a way that embodies the presence of God. It is dropping all that is "yours" and walking alongside others. It's slowing your pace of life enough to recognize others' needs. By entering into the lives of others, making trust a priority in our relationships, listening more than we talk, and consistently inviting genuine dialogue, we develop into people who care for and connect with others in a humble way—as Jesus did.

Revealing Truth: Our lives should declare the truth about God and ourselves. We are called to make known who God is, what he has done for humanity, and how to enter into a relationship with him. We share this message not merely through the spoken word but by exercising justice—standing for fairness, equality, and the honoring of all people. When we engage in spiritual conversations, share our personal stories in light of the story of God, and respond to needs in acts like giving food to the hungry, care to the ill, joy to the mourning, and clothes to the unclothed, we share God's truth and are used of God to help restore the world. In such actions, we move beyond meeting an occasional need as our schedule permits and into lives that reveal the very character of Christ.

Principle 3: Real love and service spring from "desire" rather than "duty."

We all know Christians who serve others because they think that is what Christians are "supposed" to do, not because it is what they long to do. Are you one of those people? I am trying not to be one anymore. For years I did some parts of my work with students only because I though it was my duty to do so—and the youth recognized it within me.

When I was at a church in New York, we regularly went to the Ronald McDonald House to play with the children, serve the families, clean up, and whatever else they needed us to do. We went there because it was an easy activity for me to plan, it was not far from the church (so I didn't need to arrange transportation), and it was near one of my favorite pizza places. Wrong motives? You bet they were the wrong motives! I was motivated to take these students to serve out of duty, not a desire to equip them for ministry. The same can be said for the reasons I do some other things for people. But I'm learning to move beyond acting out of obligation and seeking instead to invest myself in becoming a Jesus-like servant to all those around me. I understand that I cannot possibly do everything for everyone, but I can certainly shift my priorities to think of others more than myself.

If we want students to serve out of desire rather than duty, they must recognize the love for others that we demonstrate. As a result the love we share with others will spread like wildfire as youth begin to enjoy serving others for the sake of the kingdom of God, not the kingdom of self. If you and I are serving others solely out of duty, we can never expect our students to fully invest their lives in serving others.

Every day I pray that God would give me a more compassionate heart and a deeper longing to serve people out of my love for God and desire to please him. Presently, I serve more often out of obligation. In other words, I know God expects me to serve others, so I do. On the outside it may look like a passionate desire, but really it is a dutiful act. This shortfall in my heart allows me to meet needs, but never to become one who truly lives amidst the needs of my family, friends, and neighbors.

A new kind of youth ministry seeks to create students who serve out of a passionate desire, not humdrum duty. As leaders we must pray that God will instill that desire to serve within us and rid us of lives defined by duty. When students sense that passion in us, they will catch this contagious spirit and long to serve out of a genuine love for others and for God.

Principle 4: Our call is to think globally and act locally.

A few months ago I was staying at a hotel that encouraged guests to help conserve water by reusing towels and linens rather than having them changed each day. Beside the sink was a small placard that suggested that if guests in that hotel were willing to reuse their towels for an extra day or two, the hotel could save thousands of gallons of water. And if the hundreds of guests in the company's hotels around the world were willing to do the same, it could make a huge difference. It occurred to me that the hotel's inviting vision was not only a good way to save water but also a good way to save money! Washing fewer towels and sheets would save not only water but also time employees would spend washing laundry, electricity to run the machines, wear and tear on the machines, detergent, and more. It might save the company thousands of dollars a year.

In promoting this idea, the hotel chain used the catchphrase, "Think Globally, Act Locally." That's certainly not a new idea created by the hotel chain, but it got me thinking about the need to equip students to think globally as they act locally. We need to encourage youth to a growing awareness of the needs of the world, and what they can do in their own neighborhood to have an impact. If youth workers throughout the globe would commit to "Think Globally, Act Locally" and equip our students to do the same, we could make the world a different place!

Sound a bit idealistic? Tell that to the hotel chain that used a very old and motivating motto—regardless of whether their motivation was a genuine desire to conserve the world's natural resources or just a way to save money. I bet that campaign saved this particular hotel chain hundreds of thousands of dollars, and it changed the behavior and habits of thousands of guests worldwide. Every time guests walked into a hotel bathroom, that simple note on the sink challenged them to think about water conservation before throwing barely used towels on the floor for housekeeping to clean up.

How can you and I find ways within our ministry contexts to incorporate a global mindset—and then help students act upon it locally?

Principle 5: Stay passionate in challenging sin and injustice, while remembering God is in control.

Over the last three years I've been studying the book of Habakkuk, seeking discoveries that might help me navigate through the tragedy, sin, and injustice that surrounds us all. Habakkuk is only three chapters long, but it is full of rich and significant teaching for those following Jesus in today's world.

The literary form of the book of Habakkuk is a lament or oracle. Most other conversations between prophets and God in the Old Testament feature a message from God to be delivered through the prophet. But Habakkuk is unique in that it is the only book in the canon that is a conversation strictly between God and his prophet.

We really know very little about the prophet Habakkuk. We know he was a prophet whose name means "to embrace" and who ministered to the people of Judea under the reign of King Johoiakim, possibly during the years of 612-588 BC. Historical accounts other than the Bible tell us this was a time when the land was beset with such wickedness as idol worship, child sacrifice, and the murder of priests and prophets. Some rabbinic sources believe Habakkuk may have been the son of the Shumanite woman whom Elisha restored to life in 2 Kings 4.

Beyond that, we know very little about Habakkuk. But we dare not dismiss the significance and relevance of the book that bears his name. I believe there is much in this book that can help us navigate the tension of social injustice.

Notice first that Habakkuk fears God enough to plead to him for answers regarding the state of the land. Habakkuk's plea for God to remove the wickedness from the land is admirable and should be imitated. Habakkuk has a very clear and passionate desire to see the wickedness and injustice that surrounds him be put to an end.

Second, notice that Habakkuk's complaints remind us that we worship a God full of mystery. Habakkuk cannot figure out why God would allow his people to continue in this destruction and voices his concern. God's answers to Habakkuk remind us that God is sovereign, capable of bringing on destruction or putting a stop to it. He also reminds Habakkuk—and all of us—that it is the ongoing choices of the people to be drawn toward evil and the very traits that lead toward the wickedness.

By the time Habakkuk is done with his lament to God, he realizes his place. His role as a child of God is to be concerned with the state of the land and to do everything he can to serve the people of the land—but all the while he must remember that God is God and he is not. Habakkuk realizes his main purpose in life is to worship God and to lead the people God has entrusted to his influence to do the same.

A new kind of youth ministry seeks to instill within the hearts of all those it disciples that God is a mystery, who is just and right, and who controls the movements of the earth as he wishes. In that understanding, a new kind of youth ministry encourages the community to plead to God to restore the world from its own wickedness. But we do so with the knowledge that our chief purpose in life is to worship God, not challenge him. In that authentic worship, a new kind of youth ministry equips students to live within the tension of cultural immorality, daring not to find comfort in it but reaching toward God to find comfort in him.

God has put within our hearts a yearning to see an end to wickedness and injustice. Yet we must also realize the sovereignty of God, and rest within that rule. Resting within the rule of God does not mean that we sit back and do nothing about the wickedness and injustice. Certainly not—we are, after all, the agents of restoration God is using to bring his world back to its original condition. But we are on this earth to worship God. Maybe before we scream injustice and wickedness and point a finger here or there, we ought to worry about our own lives. Maybe we should heed Habakkuk's wise choice to declare God as God and not himself, and begin to help God restore the world by the way we live out and declare his love.

Seeking to live amidst the needs of others gives us the time and proximity we need to establish trusting relationships and declare the righteousness of God by the way we live. As directors we must reculture our ministries to allow and encourage our students to live faithfully in response to the needs that surround us, thereby declaring God's love and grace for all people.

FOR REFLECTION AND DISCUSSION:

- Does your ministry teach students simply to meet needs or do you invite them to enter into the lives of others and live amidst their needs?

- Do your students have an "us" and "them" mentality? If so, what can you do to break down this kind of thinking?

- How can your team encourage students to begin with the question, "How can I help?"

- What are some creative ways that you can teach and model what it means to develop a kingdom perspective, become a humble presence, and reveal truth?

- Do your students serve out of "duty" or "desire"?

- How are you like Habakkuk?

4 RECULTURING STUDENT LEADERSHIP

From a Few Leaders to a Community of Contributors

I don't know one youth pastor who doesn't recognize the great responsibility and privilege of helping students progress with their gifts, talents, and abilities so they can reach their potential. Nor have I ever come into contact with a youth ministry that doesn't—in some way, shape, or form—have a "student leadership team." This leadership team is usually comprised of youth who meet the following criteria:

1) They are believers

2) able to share a gospel presentation

3) willing to share their faith stories in public

4) able to attend all leadership team meetings

5) supported in their participation by consenting parents or guardians

6) willing to serve in a formal way within the youth ministry

7) willing to sign a covenant representing their desire to grow

8) eager to help the adult leaders with any and all tasks associated with building the ministry.

I have utilized student leadership teams in each year of my own ministry. During my first few years as a youth pastor, I stood firm on all of the above criteria. I confess that I tended to think of the student leadership team as a source of cheap labor. Through what I would call the middle years of my ministry, I began to see student leaders less as a labor force and more as a team of fellow ministers, and I got a little lax with some of the criteria. Now I have come to a place where I stand firm on one or two of the above criteria. But the bigger shift is that I see my role as one of developing a community of contributors who share in the mission of God, not necessarily one of building leaders.

A new kind of youth ministry seeks to invest in and influence not just those students who typically see themselves as leaders, but also the many who do not normally view themselves as leaders. I think the word *leader* makes most teenagers shake and shiver. And I think their fear is based less in their presuppositions about what leadership is than in a distrust and skepticism spawned by their own wounds. By the time most children reach adolescence, they have often had the unfortunate and tragic experience of learning that key leaders in their own lives are not, in fact, at all the people they have claimed to be. Because of the often very public scandals surrounding the church, its leaders, and its adherents, many youth distrust almost anyone who claims to be an authority or leader—for good reason.

I'm fortunate to have had good parents, good teachers and coaches, good mentors, and good pastors along the way of my journey. Of course, there have been a few authority figures in my life who have made asinine decisions that sent my world into a tailspin for a season. But generally I have been fortunate to be able to trust those around me.

Unfortunately, this generation of students, generally speaking, has not been so fortunate. They live in an age where many people in positions of authority and leadership in the church and in our world (parents, pastors, youth pastors, presidents, teachers, etc.) have not exactly been model citizens with a commitment to morality and justice. Perhaps this generation of students is no more bruised, bloodied, and crippled by the unfortunate actions of those in positions of influence as any previous generation. But the very public nature of the failings of our leaders has shaped this generation like none before it. The youth of today are a very skeptical group of maturing adults who see themselves only responsible to and for themselves. Most of these young people are very wary of anyone who claims to be a leader—or who tells them they need to become leaders. I don't think one needs to be a sociologist to grasp this common and growing trend among the emerging generations.

I certainly have not given up on today's young people for their views about us. I think for the most part that we have a tremendous population of capable, passionate, and intelligent emerging youth who long to make the world a better place. And I think the church can make that possible by offering them an environment of steadfast support, enduring trust, and unfailing love. But it seems to me that a vast majority of the students (in North America anyway) long to contribute to make this positive and meaningful contribution—*without being a leader.*

For this reason, I think that a youth ministry committed to developing contributors will be much more effective than building leaders. Furthermore, I'd speculate that this clear distinction that students draw between being contributors and leaders is not all bad. The distinction might just be what transforms the church from a corporation of leaders into a community of servants.

Before I go any further, let me acknowledge that I know there will always be individuals who are considered leaders. There will always be students in our ministries who stand out as influencers or leaders. Too often, we youth pastors have tended to focus all our attention on these potential leaders—perhaps in the hopes that their growth might extend to the larger group. But I believe this tendency has hurt the church and its young people.

Not every person has the gifts to guide a coalition, direct and manage others, serve as a principle decision maker, and be an example for others to follow meticulously. Students who don't manifest these leadership gifts undoubtedly need our intentional attentiveness as well.

I am not suggesting that we move entirely from a "few" to "the masses." If your ministry has hundred of kids—or even dozens of kids—it's impossible to develop deep relationships with every single one. I am suggesting, however, that rather than focusing all of our energy and time on the "cream of the crop," we look to balance our energy and time in efforts that attend to the entire crop. A new kind of youth ministry seeks to lead all the students in its sphere of influence to become contributors in God's mission to restore the world.

You might say, "Of course. I make sure I am attending to the whole group. That is what separates a youth group from a youth ministry!" Then why are so many youth graduating Jesus and the church when they graduate high school? Why are so few students investing time in the work of the church presently? Why are we seeing fewer and fewer youth commit to a life of vocational ministry?

Let's face it. There are very few youth pastors who devote the majority of their time to thinking strategically about how the least committed students in our ministries can take a step toward deeper commitment. We are far more likely to spend most of our time within the student leadership context, helping our most committed students become more committed. I'm not saying this is bad or wrong. But I don't think it's the most effective way to see the world change through the transformation and action of the global church community.

A new kind of youth ministry moves beyond "building leaders" and toward "developing contributors" as its primary theme. It seeks to make disciples who make disciples by being more intentional in the way it ministers to its entire community. It requires youth ministers who are eager to invest in youth with leadership gifts but also fully attentive to the importance of shepherding the full flock.

Consider the following ways you might more intentionally focus on ministering to all the youth in your care:

1. A new kind of youth ministry helps students determine who God has created them to be before determining what they need to become.

For too many years, I wasted time pushing students to dig into the bag of "achievable skills" and grab those skills that were uniquely theirs. I tried hard—too hard at times—to match the personality and makeup of my students to the gifts, talents, and skills I hoped they'd develop for serving God by the time they graduated my ministry. Although I realized that the young people needed time to grow into who they would become for Christ, I did everything

I could think of to get them started on the journey of becoming multipliable disciples.

I have discovered that, in my insane and driven need to produce quality leaders, I jumped over the most important part of helping students develop as disciples: Young people need to discover who they are *in* God before they can discover who they might become *for* God.

Too often youth ministries—and churches, for that matter—do not allow time for followers of Jesus to fully realize what it means to be children of God. We want so badly for new followers to be discipled and "fully trained" (Luke 6:40) that we do not properly teach or give time for them to wander about in the mysteries of God. But it's only in encountering these very same mysteries of God that we find the keys to unlock who we are in his creation.

Let us not be so quick to give students the skills we think they need and, by doing so, hinder them from the greatest insight into their entire being. Rather than just developing workers who can apply their specific abilities to everyday life, let us help them discover the wonder of who they are: unique individuals created by God in God's own image. Let's remind them of their own identity as children of God, united with a vast and diverse creation, yet with a unique soul, spirit, and purpose essential to the entire created order. Let us help students first know who they are; only in that awareness can they focus on what they need to become to utilize their gifts and abilities.

2. A new kind of youth ministry seeks to bring balance and equal prioritization of the gifts of the Spirit.

Walk down the hallway of most multistaffed churches and you will most likely read labels on the various office doors such as Senior Pastor, Executive Pastor, Youth Pastor, Worship Pastor, Children's Pastor, or Pastor of Leadership Development. There's nothing wrong with labels and job titles—the church has been assigning staff to specific areas of focus or age groups for years. Perhaps that is not the best way to assign staff, but it's the most common. The question I have when walking through such churches is, "Where is the office of the Pastor of Hospitality and Mercy?" Or "Where does the Pastor of Discernment and Utterances of Wisdom work?" Why do we elevate the gifts of teaching, administration, and leadership? Are those gifts more important for the church—or just more important in the minds of those who possess them? Why does the church have such a hard time balancing all of the gifts and bringing equality to the people who have them?

When churches operate as if the three gifts of teaching, leadership, and administration are primary, it's not surprising that youth ministries follow suit. In doing so, we limit the number of contributors of the mission of God to only a few. It is not helpful when we misdiagnose a person's gifts, but it's even more damaging when we altogether fail to recognize the gifts of some people. A new kind of youth ministry seeks to bring balance to the church through appreciating all of the gifts, and leaving room for students to uncover the undertaught and underappreciated gifts in their own lives.

Even if you believe certain gifts mentioned in the Scriptures are no longer active today, there are plenty of gifts that enrich the church in addition to teaching, leadership, and administration. Gifts like mercy, support, and hospitality are every bit as essential to the body of Christ. We must make our youth ministries places where these gifts are recognized and encouraged.

3. A new kind of youth ministry places emphasis on dreaming what one can do for God, not just entering into someone else's dream.

Inspiring our students to dream is critical to the vibrancy and relevancy of Christianity. Allowing space for and encouraging students to hope, long for, and make real their dreams is critical—even if those dreams seem impractical or difficult to accomplish. Our cheering students on as they imagine new ways they might be used of God is imperative not only to the growth of each student, but to the growth of the church as a whole.

A former student of mine named Kim shared one of her dreams for ministry in a recent e-mail:

> ...Currently, I'm double-majored in Youth Min and Psych, but I'm dropping Psych. That way I can graduate next year. Crazy, huh? I'll be 20 years old, armed with a 4-year degree to work with people 2 years younger than I. Then I'll either get my Psych degree from a U or a masters in Communication. Long term, I'd like to start a ministry and be a youth speaker holding conferences around the nation. I even have a name for it! Generation Jacob Ministries—People in search of the face of God. It's based on Psalm 24:6. I'm getting ahead of myself, I know, but I get excited and dream big!...

I lead a ministry that holds conferences around the nation. I'm very aware of how hard it is to develop a team of people to help with such work, develop a client base of people who will come to the events, and maintain the relationships that get established when they attend. It is very difficult to enter into a market already saturated with nonprofit ministries and organizations, as well as for-profit companies. Sometimes it hardly seems possible. But am I going to steal Kim's dream away from her? Am I going to tell her that her goal is impossible and she should find a new dream?

No! Of course I am not going to do that. First, you don't know Kim. She is one of the most passionate and gifted young contributors to the mission of God I've ever met. If anyone can break into the world of national ministry organizations, she can! Second—and maybe even more significant—who died and left me to play God? I have no idea how God will use us to continue to reveal his kingdom and restore his world. The best thing I can do is be real with Kim, help her be aware of the many challenges she will face, and decide how I can encourage and equip her along the way.

My brother once told me he was going to be a professional golfer. I told him he would never make it. He proved me wrong—

laughing all the way to the bank the entire time. I told one of my friends he would never fulfill his dream of reaching Antarctica. He proved me wrong, too. In fact, he is currently in Antarctica studying the polar ice sheets and making vital contributions to the increasingly important conversations about global warming. I once told one of my students he didn't have the grades to get into medical school or the stick-to-itiveness to become a doctor. Well, let's just say that if you are ever looking for a really good M.D., I know one I could recommend.

In Mike Yaconelli's book, *Dangerous Wonder* (Zondervan, 1998), I found a quote that has challenged me to think about how I encourage (or discourage) my students from their dreams. Mike writes, "Somewhere along the way we had the child chased out of us. Our childlikeness is usually snuffed out by people who tell us what we can't do. They are dream stealers."

I regret that I may have stolen some people's dreams over the years, perhaps because I was never much of a dreamer myself. I dream now—but growing up I never had the self-confidence to think I would ever really be used by God in a significant way. This lack of self-confidence led me to be jealous of others, and that jealousy caused me to be intentionally difficult in helping people realize their dreams. I often imagine what I might have done to help people realize their dreams and then be able to share in the joy of their achievement. Instead, I've too often been the guy who said the dream was impossible, and then was proven wrong—a rather humbling position. But I'm learning to dream big—and learning to encourage others to strive for the dreams God has placed in their hearts.

A new kind of youth ministry places a priority on developing disciples who dare to dream of new ways that can contribute to the mission of God. Such a ministry recultures itself from within to allow for all students—whether they see themselves as leaders or not—to realize who they are in God, explore all the gifts of the Spirit, and dream God-sized dreams. Rather than training a small corps of student leaders, a new kind of youth ministry invests its time in developing a wide community of disciples, eager to offer their diverse gifts in support of God's mission of restoring the world.

FOR REFLECTION AND DISCUSSION:

- How do your students respond when you call them to lead? Do your students have a reaction to the term *leader*?

- Does your ministry focus too much on its leadership oriented students? How can you place more emphasis on calling all of your youth to contribute to God's mission?

- What is the difference between "building leaders" and "developing contributors"?

- Does your ministry give equal prioritization to the spiritual gifts? What can you do to affirm those gifts your students have that might normally receive less attention?

- Do you and your leaders encourage students to dream, or do you discourage their dreams? What are some of the dreams you are hearing from your youth? How can those dreams shape your ministry?

5 RECULTURING MISSION

From Taking Trips to Living Missionally

Like many of you, I've been on my fair share of what are traditionally called "short-term mission trips." For the most part, the trips I've been on have been good learning experiences. As I recall various trips, I can easily remember some of the lessons I've learned: how to remain calm when the itinerary gets all screwed up; how to lean on God when my comfort zone is stretched; how to deal with difficult people; and how to handle life in a foreign country when half of your group will be without their luggage for a few days. I've also been moved emotionally as I saw the conditions that much of the world lives in. All of these experiences have shaped me in positive ways.

Unfortunately, when I reflect on these trips, I don't remember nearly as well the names, faces, and stories of the people we "impacted," the customs and language of the culture we were visiting (except maybe what we experienced on our "free" day), or the specific ways we cared for people. I think it's revealing (and quite troubling) that I'm easily able to remember the instances and experiences that personally affected me and those who accompanied me on the trips, but not the particulars of the very people whom we hoped to "reach for Jesus."

What would you say if a parent, volunteer, or church leader asked why you take your students on mission trips? How would you explain the hundreds, or thousands, or—for some of you—tens of thousands of dollars you spend to take your students on a mission trip? I am surprised that in over a decade of leading youth ministries I was never asked that question—not even once. I am glad I was never asked that question, because I'd have offered a poor answer at best. I am quite sure I would have responded to the question "Why do you take students on mission trips?" with one of the following comments:

- "To introduce people to Jesus…"

- "To take my students out of their comfort zone…"

- "To educate people with the truths of the Bible…"

- "To give our students a cross-cultural experience..."

- "To build community within our group..."

- "To help our students learn how to travel out of country..."

- "To see if any of our students feel called to full-time missions..."

- "To expose our students to the 'real' world..."

- "To keep balanced our ministry strategy of evangelism, discipleship and ministry training..."

- "To obey the Great Commission..."

I'm not saying these are all bad reasons to take students on mission trips. There certainly is nothing wrong with introducing people to Jesus, giving your students an experience outside their own culture and comfort zones, pushing them to consider full-time missions, or fulfilling the Great Commission. These are all good things. But they are not, in my opinion, the primary reasons to take students on mission trips.

What if we came to a new understanding about missions—one where our principal reasons for cross-cultural mission trips were not focused developing our own youth. What if we could honestly answer the "Why mission trips?" question by stating:

- "To join God in his mission to restore the world..."

- "To love people in accord with the Great Commandment..."

- "To heal brokenness, hurt, pain, confusion, and doubt..."

- "To bring dignity to the undignified..."

- "To clothe the unclothed..."

- "To bless the exploited..."

- "To care for the sick..."

- "To be Jesus..."

You get the point? If not, here it is: The primary purpose for mission trips should not be for us! It is not to see if we can shock our students with the life and experiences of the poor and needy in order to "wake up" our students. Why do we operate in such a way that our youth ministry mission trips seem designed primarily for the impact in the lives of our own students? Is that really what missions are all about?

I realized that I needed to reculture the way our youth ministry practiced missions on the way home to Minneapolis after one of our mission trips. We'd taken a few dozen youth to Nashville, Tennessee, to serve the homeless. To be honest, we really didn't do much serving. I mean we fed them, passed out clothes, and played board games with them—but we didn't really *serve* them. I say that because we did those kind things not so much out of love for these people but for the purpose of trying to inject the gospel message into our interactions with them. I confess that I'd lined up those experiences with the homeless primarily to see if my students could articulate the neat and polished gospel presentation we'd been working on for weeks. If one or two of the homeless people were persuaded to accept Jesus as their personal savior—well, that would be a bonus. At that point in my life I thought the way you prepared students for a life of ministry to the world was by giving them a compact, glossy presentation of the gospel to tell someone else. Forget about really entering into the life of another person and building a relationship over time that was worthy of having conversations about their destiny. This trip was about teaching my students to share their faith.

Anyway, after about ten days of this mediocre ministry, we were traveling home. We were about halfway back to Minneapolis when we stopped the entire caravan in Paducah, Kentucky, so we could refuel the vans. I pulled into the station, stopped the engine, and gave the students the "be back in ten minutes or we are leaving without you" speech—all the while knowing that we'd be there for at least 30 minutes. While refueling I noticed that a very similar caravan headed in the other direction was pulling into the station. As the vans got closer I read the name of a church along the side of one—a United Methodist church from Nashville.

As soon as the drivers of the caravan began to step out of their vehicles, I spotted the other youth pastor. She was the one yelling, "Be back in ten minutes or we're leaving without you!" I smiled at her and, noticing our caravan, she smiled back, realizing I was the one leading our troop. Here we were in the middle of the summer heat standing at an all-too-familiar place: a fuel pump, away from our families, each of us already having surpassed any reasonable operating stress level and now working with a very short fuse. But we were connected by our shared experience.

"How's it going?" I said.

"Okay", she said in a long, drawn-out fashion with a slight shake of her head. "Where are you headed?" she asked.

"We are going back home to Minneapolis," I said.

"Really? We just spent a week in Minneapolis!" she remarked.

"What were you doing up in our stomping grounds?" I asked.

Her response blew my mind: "We were on a mission trip—serving the homeless." Before I could say anything, she asked, "Where are you coming from?"

"We are coming off a ten-day trip of serving the homeless in Nashville."

"No way!" she exclaimed. At about the same time we looked at each other and said, "What's wrong with this picture?"

For most of the next eight hours, until we pulled into the church parking lot to the relief of dozens of waiting parents, I thought about the last ten days. I thought hard about my motives in setting up the trip, our efforts on the trip, our intentions during the trip, and the impact we may or may not have had on the people we met in Nashville. Most of all, I thought about what I was going to do to be sure that any further mission trips I led as youth pastor were going to be different. And I was going to start by rethinking what it means to "do missions."

RECULTURING YOUR MISSION DESIGN

Not long after the trip to Nashville, my staff and I sat down and began to talk about missions. We discussed the topic for days, and I discovered I wasn't the only one on our team who had concerns about our current approach to student missions.

When you are considering change, it's always important to start by getting a clear picture of your current context. Before we could consider any significant change in our approach, we had to identify current realities and assumptions regarding student missions in our church culture. We discovered the following through our context assessment:

- Our church has a rich heritage of student missions. Any changes in our mission endeavors would have to be communicated well.

- Our congregation—especially the parents of our youth—viewed the purpose of student missions in the same way I'd been viewing them—believing the experiences were first about changing *our* students and only secondarily about serving others.

- The elders assumed there would always be several student mission opportunities each summer. It would not be easy to implement a radically different model.

- Parents wanted their youth to "see the world" (without joining the Navy) and they were expecting the church (namely the youth ministry) to provide opportunities to do so through mission trips.

- The pastor of global outreach expected that youth ministry staff would embrace his view of missions as the resident expert and that our trips really should be an extension of his ministry. This would normally be no big deal, except that he was thinking of reculturing the church's mission efforts at the same time we were.

- Local mission opportunities in the Twin Cities were not considered nearly as significant as those that required traveling out of state—or better yet, applying for a passport and hopping on a plane.

- Many of our volunteers, who had shared the leadership of many of the trips, thought what we were doing was great and that there really was no need for significant change.

We also found there were differing opinions among our staff as to what student missions was all about. Not all of my staff agreed with my ideas, which is fine—disagreement can lead to productive dialogue that can be great for change. But as we talked, a number of us came to similar conclusions about the directions we wanted to pursue. We decided the time was right to reculture our approach to student missions.

After several days of discussion, we had developed a significant list of changes we hoped to see. Many of them involved a fairly major shift from an old way of thinking about missions to a brand new way:

FROM	TO
"Missions are primarily about life change within our students."	"Missions are about a genuine love for God and those we seek to serve."
"We have something superior to offer you."	"We have something to learn from you."
"Mission means a distance traveled."	"Mission means a lifestyle developed."
"Speaking about Jesus."	"Sharing and revealing Jesus in all that we do."

There were other changes we wanted to make. We wanted to dismantle the idea—in the minds of students, parents, and others—that those youth who participate in our mission trips are more spiritual than those who do not. We wanted to remove the longstanding idea that a student who accepts a call to full-time missions is in some way more important than a student who follows a more normative life path in serving God. We wanted to add opportunities for multigenerational mission experiences in which families could share in the learning.

Finally, we wanted our mission efforts to be more concerned with our intention to serve, and less with finding the most inventive or innovative trip possible.

Slowly, my team and I began to drop hints that student mission endeavors were soon going to be different. I met with "key" parents (you know, the ones that make all the noise and/or are esteemed by other parents), talked with the elders and pastors, interviewed some of the students, and talked with volunteers. The more I talked with others, the more certain I was that reculturing our emphasis in missions wasn't going to be an easy task. In fact, it became clear that pushing a new and more intentional design for missions could potentially cost me my job.

I vividly remember one particular conversation. I was sitting on the couch in the common area of our church one Sunday morning, sipping a cup of coffee and talking with some students between the two morning services. Out of the corner of my eye, I saw the mom of one of my students headed determinedly in my direction. Pretending I didn't notice her panic-stricken expression, I continued my conversation with the students seated around me. She interrupted by saying, "Chris. We need to talk!"

I turned to her and said, "I am almost done here. Can you wait a minute or two?"

"No." She sharply stated. "The service is going to start any minute and I want to find a good seat. We need to talk *now.*"

I replied as graciously as I could, "Well, then let's connect after the service or, better yet, let's connect over the phone sometime this week."

"This cannot possibly wait," she claimed. She waited impatiently for me to finish my conversation. I asked the mom to have a seat. She proceeded to rip into me, accusing me of everything from ruining her daughter's once in a lifetime opportunity to go on an overseas mission trip to being a pluralist to being soft on hell. I responded as calmly as I could, trying to help her see that what we were trying to do in shifting our traditional mission trips was not going to destroy the experience for the students. In fact, I argued, the changes would enhance the experience by helping them realize the difference between going on a mission trip and living a missional life.

She didn't really buy it. She concluded our conversation (now more than halfway through the service she "couldn't miss") by saying, "I'll be having a conversation with our pastor about this. I am extremely disappointed in you and your wife." Before I even had time to ask what my wife had to do with any of this, she walked away angrily—and has never spoken to me again.

Reculturing is hard work. It takes patience, tough skin, and the ability to forgive (and sometimes forget). It takes a sharp mind (I usually draft off the minds of those around me!), as well as a heart and passion big enough to navigate and lead change. Most of all, it takes dependence on God for strength to endure. Reculturing can be a lot like a contact sport—it will tackle you, punch you in the gut, pull your muscles, run past you, hit you with its fastball, check you into the boards, throw you off its back, dunk on you, and make you want to retire early. Are you up for it?

FROM MISSION TRIPS TO LIVING MISSIONALLY

In reculturing our mission emphasis, we weren't simply hoping to offer students a different kind of mission trip—although that certainly was part of what we were seeking to do. Ultimately, we were hoping our mission trips would be times of service that would inspire students to *missional living* in their everyday lives.

We began to redesign our ministry's mission model around our understanding of Acts 1:8, the familiar call to "be witnesses in Jerusalem, Judea, Samaria, and the uttermost parts of the world." Rather than hearing this as a call to distant cities, we encouraged students to embrace the idea that, wherever they might be in the world, they are called to be witnesses to God's restorative plan. Missional living is not about what one does on the occasional trip to a far-off place. It is a way of living at home, at school, and in our everyday lives—wherever God places us.

Over the last few years, the term *missional living* has been a part of the emerging church's vocabulary. I love the term—though I'm not sure I completely understand all of its connotations and what it means for my life and community. But the basic idea is that we followers of Jesus are to live as active "missionaries" among all with whom we may interact throughout the journey of life. Missional living is in most contexts a "new" way in which to approach our lives. The term is intended to push people to live like Jesus (living incarnationally) regardless of profession, cultural context, geographic location, or situation. Missional living is similar to the life-dynamic approach to evangelism discussed in Chapter One in that it is about a Spirit-filled engagement with

the life unfolding around us, joining God in what he is already doing rather than what he might use us to do. Take a moment to ponder what Erwin McManus, the founder and pastor of Mosaic in southern California, had to say about missional living.

It is why the church exists. The key to the missional church is to love more profoundly and more deeply. It is not "having" a mission, but "being" God's mission: God's alternative people who signify God's reign over all is what lies at the heart of the missional church.

BLUR
Adam Hendrix
www.bluryourlife.com

Blur is an intensive weeklong event in Seattle in which students are challenged to a life without compartments. At Blur, students are pushed to take their relationship with God beyond the facts and into deserted corners of their life. It is an exercise in missional living.

Blur gives students a packed week of training by experienced Jesus-followers, ministry experience in both urban and suburban contexts, intense times of prayer in both traditional and creative settings, times of meditation and reflection, group-building activities, and more—all for the purpose of helping students move beyond the idea of "doing missions" and instead learn what it means to live as a missionary.

Consider the differences between doing missions and missional living:

"Doing Missions"	"Living Missionally"
I take part in our congregation's annual mission trip each summer— or support others who do.	I am a missionary—every day.
I separate the sacred and the secular—for example, my special opportunity to serve God on an occasional mission trip and my normal role as a husband/wife or father/mother.	I recognize that God is working in all of life, and because of that I seek to work in all of life with Him.
I think real missions are best left to "called missionaries."	I believe we are all called to be missionaries.
I think mission endeavors happen cross-culturally.	I live in a cross-cultural mission context.
I am Great Commission oriented.	I am Great Commandment and Great Commission oriented.
I do not have the skills or gifts to be a missionary.	God has created me with unique gifts that I can use on behalf of his mission.
The church supports missionaries and mission projects.	The church lives out God's mission.

I am sure there are a number of other distinctive elements of missional living that exemplify its divergence from doing missions. As I mentioned earlier, I am only at the point of discovering what missional living means. The most important question probably isn't, "What are the many differences between the two?" The question for us to grapple with is, "How do we get students to discover, investigate, and function within a missional life?"

DEVELOPING STUDENTS WHO LIVE MISSIONALLY

I don't believe there is any secret formula we can follow to develop students who live missionally. But there are some practical steps we can take as shepherds of our ministry to help nurture students toward missional living.

It might seem obvious, but the first and perhaps the most important step we can take in helping others live missionally is to be consistently moving toward that goal ourselves. With the same amount of passion and energy that students use to sniff out inauthentic behavior in us, they can also be inspired to take action when they see us living missionally with authenticity and integrity. This means our everyday behaviors should reflect the characteristics of living missionally noted in the chart above. If we are not living it, we can't expect or even call our students to live it.

A second step is to help our students understand that the world was not created for them but that instead they are to care for and look after all of God's creation. Caring for the world means to be concerned not with how humanity enjoys creation but how we steward it.

Not long ago I led a small group of students and adult leaders to the top of a mountain in the Black Hills of South Dakota. It wasn't a particularly long or demanding hike, but the point of this particular hike was not to push the group to exhaustion. The point was to get to the top, have a conversation about the beauty that we could see all around us, and then worship together. There was no worship band nor any elaborate moving images behind song

MERGE
Sonlife Ministries
www.sonlife.com/merge

Merge is a weeklong experience held in 5 different North American cities where high school students are challenged to merge with God's story by gaining a deeper understanding of the great, overarching story of God. Students are invited to merge with God's way of life by discovering through the story what God is like and how we were created to live. Merge also seeks to help students merge with God's mission by realizing their role in the great story as part of a faith community that brings God's love and restoration to the world.

lyrics flashed up on a screen— just us and God and his creation. Our service was built around praising God for his creation and challenging our students and adult leaders to care for it. It was one of the most wonderful worship times I have ever experienced—and I know that many in our group felt similarly. Years later, students still ask me if I remember the view and our conversation at the top in which I called them to remind themselves daily that this world and everything in it is God's and that God has chosen us to look after the creation while he lets us live here for a while.

Another practical step we can take to help guide and nurture our students toward a missional life is to help break down the common misunderstanding that there is a particular skill-set required to serve as a missionary. God knew exactly what he was doing when he created each one of us. We were all created to be agents of restoration. Each of us has a unique role to play in contributing to God's mission. When we have a mission team that's leaving for their intended location, we often pray a prayer of commissioning over them but at the same time pray a prayer of commissioning over those who are staying in town and not attending the mission trip. Even if most of the students intend to spend their summer serving ice cream, mowing lawns, babysitting, whatever the case might be, they get a prayer of commissioning as well. That very simple yet very profound action means a lot to the students who are "staying home." Try it next time you are sending a team on a mission trip. You might be surprised at the impact it has on the students who might otherwise see themselves as missing out or not special enough to be a part of God's mission.

Speaking of mission trips, I was asked during a recent seminar if I even thought mission trips were helpful anymore. Perhaps you are wondering the same thing. I do think mission trips are helpful—if they have the right motivation and accomplish the purpose of truly sharing and showing Jesus.

Most youth workers I know love to take students out of their "comfort zone" on mission trips—and that is all well and good. To me, however, the point of going on a mission trip—whether it's to a distant land or to your local homeless shelter—is not about getting your kids outside their comfort zones. Rather, it is about loving people in a way that embodies Jesus. You say that you want to motivate students to be Jesus in a context other than their own? Great. I applaud that. But I think the bigger challenge is to find ways to encourage our youth to consistently be Jesus in the mundane, easy, and ordinary context of their lives, not just in those infrequent and extraordinary moments of life. I'm not sure we can assume that just by challenging students to get out of their comfort zones on a mission trip we are really nurturing them to live missionally in their daily lives.

A new kind of youth ministry seeks to help students live their everyday lives as active missionaries and agents of God's restoration. As the shepherd of your ministry (or at least one of the shepherds), you'll need to determine whether your current efforts are effectively helping students live missionally based on your ministry context. If you decide that change is required, be absolutely intentional about the change your ministry is undertaking. Make sure that your change efforts are rooted in biblical intentions and not just the desire for invention and innovation. Don't employ what is hip, trendy, or flashy; employ what is effective, impacting, and transformational.

FOR REFLECTION AND DISCUSSION:

- What kind of mission trips does your ministry lead? What do your students take from these trips?

- What is the difference between doing missions and living missionally? How can you create opportunities and shape environments to help students understand the difference?

- What are some characteristics of missional living? How can your ministry better encourage students to live missionally in their everyday lives?

- What seems most exciting about the possibility of reculturing your mission efforts? What seems most discouraging or scary?

6 RECULTURING LEADERSHIP

From Going It Alone to Ministry Partnerships

Over the last ten years I have grown as a leader. But that growth process hasn't been driven primarily by reading books with 21 laws, attending summits on becoming a dynamic leader, understanding the CEO leadership mindset, or even through mentoring relationships. The primary way I've discovered what it takes to be a leader has been through my own screwups—and I have had plenty of them.

I recall one parents meeting when I learned a ton about what it means to lead. One parent, a regular and really good antagonist, stood up to challenge a few of my plans for the year. After about ten minutes of listening to her pleading her case as to why my every plan needed to be readjusted to respect the particular schedule and needs of her family, I lashed out angrily at her saying, "This church is not here just for your family!" In front of about 75 parents, I had taken the embarrassment other parents felt about her and her outlandish requests and redirected their focus onto me and my angry statement.

My wife was in the room at the time, and she just lowered her head and closed her eyes. She knew I was right in telling this parent that the church wasn't here on this planet just to serve her family, and that sometimes that meant her kids might have to miss some activities and events so others could attend. But my wife also knew this was another case where my mouth was getting me into trouble. Actually, it wasn't my mouth at all—my mouth was just a symptom of the problem.

The real problem was that I had a very narcissistic and flawed perspective on leadership. I thought that leading a youth ministry meant I was in charge. I thought the ministry should revolve around my own vision, gifts, and preferred direction. I caused a lot of hurt and indignity before some folks who could see my potential but also my problems helped me discover a new perspective on leadership.

Until a few years ago I led my youth ministries as top-down organizations. After all, I was the trained professional, hired to serve as the youth minister. It took me quite awhile to learn that leadership doesn't come with a position, leadership comes with the ability to influence others. And you can't influence others if you are such a jerk that no one wants to be around you. As a famous proverb goes, "If you think you are leading, and you look behind you and no one is following, think again. You are really just out for a long, lonely walk."

In recent years I have worked hard to reculture my own leadership paradigm from one focused on my personal preferences and style to one that is marked by genuine ministry partnership. Consider the following discoveries I've made about leading in the context of youth ministry.

Discovery 1: Real leadership is not about what I do best. It is about discovering what volunteers and parents do best—and helping them find ways to contribute.

Recently I've concluded that effectively leading a youth ministry requires that I realize and rely on the abilities of those around me rather than always relying on myself. I have found that my volunteers are very capable people with a wide range of talents and skills that I could only dream about having. Finding ways to employ their gifts, talents, and abilities is central to my role as the shepherd of the ministry.

In my travels I get the chance to converse at length with youth ministry volunteers in churches across the country. They often confide that the biggest reason they do not make a solid, long-term commitment to serve the student ministries at their congregations is because they do not feel their greatest assets are being utilized. I have found that people tend to volunteer their time because of four things:

1. They sense both a calling and an opportunity to make a difference.

2. The ministry gives them a chance to do something they do well.

3. They are encouraged or empowered along the way through words, actions, and ongoing training.

4. They get to serve alongside like-minded people, which helps develop community.

A new kind of youth ministry is intentional about helping its adult volunteers discover who God has created them to be and then allowing them space and opportunity to become that person. Such ministries are committed to moving away from the personal preferences and style of the primary leader, and instead developing a spirit of genuine partnership where the gifts of the entire community are used.

Discovery 2: If we are focused on glorifying ourselves, there's not much chance we'll be glorifying God.

I used to get a real charge out of hearing the word "pastor" said in front of my name. Whenever someone addressed me as "Pastor Folmsbee" or "Pastor Chris," it was a small reminder that I was in charge and that the ministry revolved around me. When I moved to a new church that didn't have the custom of using the title "pastor," I struggled a bit to find my place as a leader. I was seeking to find my place as a leader in the position over people, not in the prospective influence of people.

I had concluded early in my first ministry opportunity that I was going to carry out programs and events that made me look like a good leader. Then, hopefully, I would find my way to a larger and more influential church that paid more. I was more concerned with making myself known and famous than with making God known or famous. This arrogance and self-centeredness pushed me to make the ministry about me, not about the students or other leaders—and definitely not about God.

When volunteers would approach me and offer ideas or constructive criticism, I would often blow it off and classify their statements under one or several categories: There was "It's not my idea so it can't be good," and "Clearly they don't have a clue about youth ministry," and "That's someone else's idea so if I implement it, it makes me look like I don't know what I am doing," and "Since I'm the youth pastor, I should come up with all the good ideas." Right now you're laughing and shaking your head, saying, "How stupid—this guy is one conceited jerk!" Well, you may be correct about that. But be careful in judging me, just in case you sometimes have similar thoughts.

Connie was one of my volunteers, and she was as arrogant as I was. Since Connie was older and more mature, she probably knew how to be a little less obvious in her arrogance. But at the end of the day, the two of us could hardly fit in the same room because our heads were so big. Connie was great for our ministry in many ways. She was extremely committed and willing to give of her own time and money. She was always asking if I needed help and offering to serve in some way. She was wonderful to have on our leadership team because she understood things like the need for change, the desire for relevance and competency, and the fact that tradition and past successes didn't always translate into an effective future.

One day Connie came into an appointment with me and said, "You are the haughtiest person I have ever known—except for myself." We laughed together at the truth of her statement. Then we looked each other in the eyes, and made an agreement that we were going to help each other grow out of our self-centeredness and grow into being more like Jesus. In that conversation Connie and I were reminded that the youth ministry we were involved with, like any other ministry inside or outside the church, is not about me, or her, or anyone else. It is not about trying to gain recognition, enhance our reputations, or feel good about ourselves. It is about surrendering ourselves to God as Jesus did and becoming an instrument that God can use to reveal his kingdom.

Do you want to be a great youth worker so you can be called great, or do you want to make God look great? Leaders must get over themselves or they never really become leaders. I often come across youth workers who say, "If I had some volunteers, we could be really effective." Sadly, in too many cases, it is the youth pastor's own ego that keeps others from wanting to participate. We can't expect others to follow until we give up our bigheadedness and begin to influence through and with a spirit of selflessness.

A new kind of youth ministry goes through the reculturing process to become a ministry driven by a genuine longing for the development of all within the ministry, not just the development of its primary leader. Someone who is intentional about making others look good for the sake of God looking great leads a God-honoring ministry.

Discovery 3: Doing all the work ourselves might make us look busy and feel satisfied, but it certainly doesn't help our ministry become more effective in fostering spiritual progress.

Youth ministers often complain about being "too busy." There are many reasons for this. In some cases there is certainly an unavoidable busyness that is caused by a ton of ministry opportunities and responsibilities. In many other cases, however, I think the business is generated from the pursuit of self.

I think the rationalized but irrational behavior of the "overworked" youth worker often has more to do with looking busy than it does being busy. Some youth workers want people to know they are busy because it brings with it statements like, "Thanks for all you are doing," or "Gosh, where would our youth be without you," or even "You've

NATIONAL LEADERSHIP TRAINING AND COACHING CENTER
Keith Cote
www.nltcc.com

The NLTCC is dedicated to the development of Christian leaders involved in student ministry around the world. Through relationships, resources and ongoing coaching, this ministry help leaders reach their full potential in all areas of their life. The NLTCC provides a unique combination of personal and ministry coaching that goes far beyond skill-set development. While helping individuals developing the skills for successful leadership is certainly part of the NLTCC mission, they are equally concerned with helping leaders better understand who they are, who they are becoming, and whom they are influencing.

been spending so much time running—why don't you take a few days off?" We do all the work so we can get all the praise. The more people think we are doing, the more pats on the back we get.

I remember one staff person who worked under me for a while. He was quite young, but mature for his age and a very gifted guy. But his somewhat sheltered upbringing and lack of ministry in the "trenches" left him a little under equipped. I took a shot on him as a contributor to our team because I recognized significant potential in his abilities and an unwavering love for students and their families.

I was pleasantly surprised after hiring him and doing ministry alongside him. He was making more of an immediate impact in the lives of students and leaders than I thought he would. He was maturing more quickly than I would have ever predicted, and I was generally thrilled with his work ethic, his initiative, his teachable spirit, and his overall contribution to our team. He had one glaring weakness though. Every time I placed him in front of our volunteers—whether it be for training, general communication, teaching, whatever—he would whine about how busy he was and how he didn't have enough time to get all of his work done. He would go on and on about how much the ministry was sucking out of him and how the volunteers were not contributing enough to the ministry.

Meanwhile, most of the people attending each of these meetings were people who were working 50 or 60 hours a week at their jobs, driving 30 minutes each way to get to the church for the meeting, trying to find childcare during the meeting, and giving 5 to 10 hours a week serving the church in some capacity! Needless to say, people didn't exactly want to follow a guy who would whine about his life being so busy when he lived two blocks from the church where he worked, didn't have any children, and was getting paid for being at the meeting! Even when volunteers tried to "save" him from his misery, he wouldn't let them take anything off his plate because he was such a control freak. I worked with him for months on his glaring weakness but to no avail. He is still serving in a youth ministry context, and continues to have a hard time engaging volunteers.

I contend that youth workers who are so busy that they have to run around like chickens with their heads cut off or stand in front of their volunteers and beg for help (and then not let them help) are not leading effectively. Good leaders know how to create a sense of "we" and develop ministry with a spirit of collaboration and partnership. A new kind of youth ministry features leaders who are intentional about creating teams, sharing the work, and creating a collective urgency to fulfill mission under the umbrella of "we," not "I".

Discovery 4: A desire for perfection in our ministries can prevent them from being effective.

I used to be so driven to see my ministry be perfect. I wanted no mistakes—and if you made one while working with me, either I wasn't doing my job well enough or you were not competent to do the job I was asking you to do. If the sound person was late to turn on the microphones, if the person doing the announcements missed one, if the worship leader had to start a song over, if the person dimming the lights did so at the wrong time, if the bus driver got lost, if the graphic designer messed up the image, if the person in charge of our Web site was late in updating it—if *anyone* did *anything* in a way that was not excellent enough, I felt I was failing in my role as a leader.

At this stage in my ministry, none of those things matter to me. Who cares if every little detail comes off without a hitch? If I am helping people serve in ways that make a difference in kids' lives, then who cares if now and then I come face-to-face with a blunder! The real blunder (and a tragic one it would be) would be if I weren't giving people a chance to serve within their gifts and interests, because of my fear that it wouldn't all be perfect.

I meet too many leaders who are panic-filled control freaks. In many youth workers' minds, nothing short of perfection qualifies as success. Just the other day I spoke at a high school assembly. Several hundred students packed an auditorium (attendance was required) to listen to a presentation about "loving the world around you." The blunders throughout this event included the video projector not working properly, the student running the slide show falling behind the teacher doing announcements, the sound system constantly feeding back, and a student cussing during the personal sharing time. By the time I got up to present my material, there had been more blunders than the latest X Games blooper video. I thought nothing of it. During my presentation the students were attentive, engaged, and seemed to really be tracking. In fact, I remember thinking to myself as I finished, "That might be the best talk I have ever done." As soon as the students were dismissed, the person who had invited me to speak ran over and said, "I am so sorry. This was a disaster."

I responded, "Really? I thought I did an okay job."

She said, "No, not you! You were great. We stunk though."

I scowled a bit, put my hand on her shoulder and said, "Relax. Today was great. What more could you have wanted?"

She said, "We made way too many mistakes this morning. This school is about helping students achieve success. We do everything we can do to help these students understand what it means to be a success in life, in their future careers, and in their future family structures. We cannot tolerate these mistakes."

I looked deep into her eyes, and noticed that they were filling with tears. I said, "You had more than a dozen students participating behind the scenes in this event this morning. You had half a dozen on the stage! Success doesn't come through assuring that these students don't make mistakes. They are not even 18 years old! They will make mistakes. That is what they do. Adolescence, for some, is one big mistake! Instead of trying to make these kids function perfectly, why don't you just be concerned with making sure they are contributing and then guide and coach them along the way?"

"We do that, too," she said. "I have to get to my class." And on that comment she turned and walked away, seemingly frustrated.

I run into many youth workers with attitudes just like this. They are pushed by their own desire to produce the perfect program or ministry. They don't seem to realize that perfection is unattainable and that we are all flawed. Therefore, they do their work under a self-inflicted anxiety that allows them very little patience and tranquility.

I understand that we are called to do our best in everything that we do. And I don't think that avoiding perfectionism should ever mean a lack of care for the ministries that have been entrusted to us. Just as perfectionism can frustrate volunteers, it can be equally frustrating for volunteers who feel like the hours they are committing are being wasted in an underachieving and static endeavor. The key is to find a balance between a God-given desire for excellence in ministry and a perfectionism that stifles ourselves and others.

A new kind of youth ministry seeks to navigate the tensions involved in being driven toward success. It works to make partnership foundational to our ministry, even when perfection and what we commonly refer to as "success" are at risk.

Discovery 5: A "you need me" mentality among leaders is clearly not as helpful as an "I need you" mentality.

Last summer I attended one of Sonlife's student ministry experiences focused on equipping students to minister to their peers. There were many youth pastors there with their students, and I tried to speak with as many of them as I could. Of course, the connecting times I usually have in these settings are all too often very similar. After the typical "So, how are you doing?" is out of the way, the youth worker usually tells me about his or her church, perhaps throwing out some numbers about the size and scope of the ministry. Many times, the youth worker will then puke out onto the table all that has him or her frustrated, confused, and concerned. In many conversations, I hear something like, "I can't believe the senior pastor treats me this way! They need me! If I just walked away from all this crap, they would all be up a creek!" or "I don't think the church realizes how good it has it. They pay horribly, put me in a basement office, give me a five-year-old computer, and expect me to do my job well? If I left, they would never get another committed youth pastor like me." Sometimes I even hear, "If it weren't for me, my church would be in a world of hurt."

I realize that many senior pastors are jealous or envious of their youth pastors. Some youth pastors are treated poorly or unfairly. And it's true that many youth workers are paid poorly, and that we are most likely to get the oldest computers and the least attractive offices. But does that really mean we can't do our jobs well? Do you really think that if you left your current position, the church would never get another committed leader for its youth ministry? Come on. Really? The church doesn't need *you*. What the church needs is a servant who is willing to embrace the community that surrounds it and intentionally nurtures students and their families in the ways of Jesus. But when any of us starts thinking he or she is indispensable, that person is in for trouble.

I carried the "you need me" attitude around for several years. I thought that every church that hired me *needed* me. The congregation didn't need a person *like me* in a position serving the families and youth of the church, it needed *me*. I couldn't have been more wrong. Leading is not about helping people realize that they need you. Leadership is about you and me serving people.

I found out over the course of several years that I am not as indispensable as I thought. As I've monitored the ongoing youth ministries of churches I've departed, I have found that the ministries keep going—and in one case, it has grown in leaps and bounds. The youth pastor that church hired to replace me is incredibly talented, and the ministry has moved far beyond where I could have led it.

The real truth is that I needed that church—and I am reminded of that fact every time I talk to a former student or colleague from that congregation. In fact, if I would have had a better perspective on leadership while I was there, I might not have ever left the church to begin with.

A new kind of youth ministry works toward developing its ministry around partnership, collaboration, teamwork, community, and shared experiences, not the primary youth pastor's personal preferences and style. Someone has to lead, and if you are the one charged with casting the vision, guarding the vision, and leading the direction of your ministry, that's great. It does not have to be about you, however. Real leaders find a way to move beyond their own self-interests and place the needs of others, and the contributions they offer, at the front of the line.

FOR REFLECTION AND DISCUSSION:

- As the leader of your ministry, do you care more about your personal preferences than the skills and abilities of others? (Answer this question yourself, and also ask for others' impressions.)

- How is your ministry doing at helping people discover who God has created them to be?

- Do you try to be too perfect in your efforts?

- How do you respond to others' mistakes and mishaps that affect your ministry? What about your own mistakes?

7

RECULTURING EDUCATION

From Teacher-Centered Curricula to Learner-Centered Environments

I have a deep admiration for teachers and other educators. Teachers are people who give of themselves to enhance someone else's abilities. The best educators often work long hours at low salaries, work through the summer even when most of us see it as their time off, and spend countless hours in a classroom. They spend their days not only interacting with a wide variety of students (many of whom would rather not be there at all) but also wrestling with the local, regional, and national politics that drive the larger educational system.

A close friend of mine named Polly Patrick is this kind of educator. She has been teaching high school students for more than twenty-five years—and not just during the typical school hours. Polly stays late into the afternoon offering students extra help, attends the extracurricular events of her students, and might even attend the wake of a student's family member. Besides her commitment to students at Minnetonka High School near Minneapolis, she serves her colleagues in a similar manner, teaching graduate level classes at St. Thomas University and the University of Minnesota. Polly doesn't put in extra hours in order to get overtime pay. She does it because she believes in shaping the lives of young people by helping them reach their potential, helping them dream dreams that have never been dreamt before and become whole citizens committed to serving the world.

In addition to being an excellent teacher, Polly is also what I would call an educational theorist. She is constantly seeking to discover new ways to help students learn. She's not looking for flashy new trends, but for innovative ways to improve the learning capacities of her students.

I believe that all of us youth workers need to see ourselves as educators. We play a critical role in providing spiritual, intellectual, and social directives for students. We serve as shepherds who guide and shape the lives of those under our care through learning experiences and opportunities.

Many of the youth workers with whom I come into contact do not recognize their important role in educating students. These youth workers think of themselves as entertainers rather than educators. Therefore, their programming is built around keeping students' attention but not helping students learn. What is the result of that? We have a continent full of youth who never learn how to be disciples of Christ. Instead of becoming developing followers of Jesus, they become only slightly aware of Jesus.

Unfortunately, even those youth workers I bump into who do see themselves as educators often entirely miss the point of education. It seems almost too obvious to say that education should be designed to enhance the knowledge, skills, and abilities of the student, not the knowledge, skills, and abilities of the teacher. As obvious as that statement is, as I interact with youth ministries all over North America, it is equally obvious to me that most youth ministries operate in a teacher-centered (or curriculum-centered) environment, not a learner-centered environment. The differences between the two educational philosophies are monumental. A new kind of youth ministry is one that is reculturing its educational programming and strategies around the learners, not the instructor.

There are a number of distinct differences between learner-centered teaching practices and those focused on teachers and curriculum. But before you read any further, you should think about whether you are willing to change your approach to educating students in your ministry. If you are unwilling to consider changes that will take you away from how you currently program your youth ministry, then skip to the next chapter now—because this one won't be all that helpful to you. But if you are open to pursuing and potentially employing a new kind of learning in your ministry, then consider the following attributes of a learner-centered educational environment.

Attribute 1: Learner-centered education is built around the needs of the students, not the preferences or skill-set of the teacher.

I find that the educational programming in many youth ministries seems focused more on the style and abilities of the youth worker than on the needs of the students. Generally speaking, most young people need interactive, dialogical, experiential, relational, and emotional involvement from the teacher in order to best learn. Many youth ministries struggle to create such a learning environment. In some cases there is an innocent lack of knowledge regarding educational techniques, but in many other cases, it is an issue of pride or fear. Most youth workers are eager to teach in ways that make them look good, feel encouraged, and build their own egos. That may sound harsh, but I think it's true. We youth workers feed off the feeling we get when we "really connect" through a God-talk or when we see students interacting in the devotional we prepared or the lesson we wrote (usually that day or the night before). But if we are going to be most effective in our attempt to change the lives of our students, we have to get beyond relying on what "works" for us and our particular "gift mix."

When I recommend this change to youth ministries that I observe and consult with, the youth pastor's reaction is usually a bit hesitant, or even negative. A lot of youth workers can't imagine the night, event, or program not revolving around their gifts. We want to feel as though we are contributing to the growth of our students—and there's nothing wrong with that, unless it prevents us from pursuing change.

Many youth workers have a hard time figuring out what it might mean to develop learning opportunities that don't focus on their own writing and teaching, because they believe these are their gifts. I can't tell you how many youth workers think they have the gift of teaching but really don't. There are those who think that because they were hired or commissioned by the church to be the youth pastor or leader, that means they have to be the one who develops and directs all the learning opportunities. That could not be further from the truth! You are called to lead the best way you can. This means you have to locate the person who is the best educator. Maybe the best educator is you—or maybe it isn't you!

I realize that some youth ministers work in situations where the senior pastor or church leaders don't see the value of a learner-centered educational environment and may insist that the youth pastor do all the teaching, devotional writing, etc. If that's your situation, you have to do what your supervisors ask you to do—but not necessarily without a hard conversation about what really will best serve the needs of the youth in your church.

Attribute 2: A learner-centered educational environment steadily evolves to meet the needs of its students, while a teacher-centered environment tends to be static and conventional in nature and content.

A learner-centered youth ministry is always evolving. It tends to be a bit more informal and less structured, but never at the expense of compromising learning. The best youth ministries are not willing to forgo true learning for the sake of what is innovative and trendy, but seek to find a balance between established techniques that have proven effective and new ideas that might work better.

A traditionally programmed youth ministry tends to be more conservative in nature (I am not referring to theological conservatism here) and more apt to stick with "what got us here" or "what works." A traditional learning environment is typically characterized by predictability, sameness, routine, structure and formality. There is usually a working agreement in traditional learning environments that long-established techniques and what is tried and true wins out over what might be new and immeasurable.

I suppose most traditional learning environments operate with a mentality of "if it ain't broke, then don't fix it." There is absolutely nothing wrong with this, as long as students are learning. But in a culture where formal educators in middle schools and high schools increasingly find that students no longer respond to traditional techniques, it is not likely that learning will be maximized in a traditional environment. You may want to speak with teachers in your area about their learning techniques or ask if you can observe a few typical middle or high school classes in your local school district. In most cases the principal or administration will let you observe, especially if you wish to learn.

Attribute 3: A learner-centered environment favors "depth" of learning over "breadth" of learning.

Learner-centered environments seek to offer students the opportunity to explore themes in depth, resulting in a deeper understanding and application. Such an approach has proven valuable in many schools, and can be equally effective in a youth ministry context.

Many youth ministries spend a little bit of time on a wide variety of topics and themes. Recognizing the limited time that's available to them, they try to touch on a range of subjects, hoping the learner will be able to interact with a host of concepts or ideas. But too often this style of teaching actually allows students to engage very little with any of the material, because they are trying to take in and interact with many concepts over a short period of time. Most youth ministries would be far better off narrowing their focus, and allowing students to delve more deeply into their subject and its applications.

For example, let's say you are planning to lead a 13-week study on the life of Jesus. One possibility would be to cover one major event in the life of Jesus each week. Your outline might look something like this:

Week 1: Prophetic Announcements concerning Jesus

Week 2: Jesus' Birth

Week 3: The Baptism of Jesus

Week 4: The Temptation of Jesus

Week 5: The Appointment of the 12 Disciples

Week 6: The Ministry of Jesus

Week 7: The Miracles of Jesus

Week 8: The Last Supper

Week 9: The Betrayal of Jesus

Week 10: The Trial and Crucifixion of Jesus

Week 11: The Resurrection

Week 12: The Appearances of the Risen Christ

Week 13: The Ascension

With only 45 minutes for each session, your best hope is that you can simply cover the basics of these events in Jesus' life. But your limited time barely gives you opportunity to introduce the various Scriptures and complementing material, and offers no time at all for the students to interact with the material in small groups, ask questions, journal what they are learning, practice retelling the stories in their own words, view or listen to media, or gaze on classic art depictions of the event. Without these more interactive learning elements, you can be sure you'll do no more than touch on the proverbial "tip of the iceberg." In the end, your students will learn very little about the life of Jesus—and even less about why that life makes a difference in their lives—despite the fact that you've spent 13 weeks studying it!

Planning like this is too often concerned with the question of "How much can we teach our students?" But the more important question is "How much will our students actually learn?" There is a big difference between these two inquiries.

So how might you cover the life of Jesus with your students in a manner that is more focused on the development of the learner rather than the content of the curriculum? What might such a planning guide look like? Consider this as a possibility:

Truth 1: The Deity of Jesus

    Week 1: The Divine Names of Jesus

    Week 2: The Divine Attributes of Jesus

    Week 3: The Divine Works of Jesus

Truth 2: The Humanity of Jesus

    Week 4: The Incarnation of Jesus

    Week 5: The Character of Jesus

    Week 6: The Priorities of Jesus

Truth 3: The Ministry of Jesus

    Week 7: The Teaching of Jesus

    Week 8: The Miracles of Jesus

    Week 9: The Atonement of Jesus

Truth 4: Our Interactions with Jesus

    Week 10: Praying with and to Jesus

    Week 11: Abiding in Jesus

    Week 12: Participating in the Suffering of Jesus

    Week 13: Following Jesus Every Day

You will notice that the series is still 13 weeks and is still focused on Jesus. What is not the same, however, is the depth of the content. I contend that a student would learn far more about Jesus (if that student is engaged) within the second of the two presented planning guides. Rather than simply giving a comprehensive but basic chronology of Jesus' life, this second plan gives the learners an intensive and profound look at who Jesus was, what he has done, and how they can interact with him. I also believe that the various and numerous life applications in the second plan will bring students to a deeper understanding of Jesus and his importance in their lives.

Neither of the two planning guides is wrong. Both will work, especially if the teaching is interactive and engaging. But a new kind of youth ministry seeks to plan around depth rather than breadth, in order to move beyond informing and focus on transforming.

Attribute 4: A learner-centered environment emphasizes experiential learning over memorization and repetition.

Many youth ministries throughout North America still design their educational programming in what might be considered a mechanical fashion. These ministries see successful learning in terms of producing students who can repeat a truth or concept. Unfortunately, such repetition does not ensure that youth actually have any real understanding of an idea's meaning or significance. Take memorizing Scripture, for example. Students learn verses by heart, can easily bring them to mind, and can often repeat long passages (sometimes even entire books) without flaw. In many cases, however, students have learned the words by heart, but have not learned what it means to live them out through the heart. Students walk away from these ministries able to quote hundreds of verses, which is not inherently bad. But is the

IMAGO MEDIA
Mark Novelli/Kelly Dolan
www.imagomedia.com

Imago Media provides video, print, and Web design as well as event planning and production for several major youth ministry organizations in North America. They have introduced imaginative new ways to create student ministry experiences through the arts, media, storytelling, writing, etc.—all for the purpose of taking students into deeper places in their faith journeys. Imago Media is assisting dozens of churches and organizations in shifting from teacher-centered to learner-centered environments. Give their blog a quick read to learn more about how Imago Media is helping churches, schools, and other organizations communicate successfully and create environments for effective ministry.

memorization of these words really helping them become more fully formed as disciples?

This is where the need for an "experiential" learning environment comes into play in most North American youth ministries. Rather than working only to help their students memorize Scripture, youth workers are seeking to develop actions out of their students' heart that reflect the significance of the Scripture. One way some ministries are doing that is by finding meaningful ways to engage the five senses as part of Scripture memory.

Jeff Holmberg is a creative arts pastor at the Soulstice Community in Minneapolis, Minnesota. Jeff is the most innovative person I know when it comes to employing creative and experiential elements into learning. Jeff doesn't seek to be flashy, trendy, or cool; his goal is to help people engage with Christian truth and concepts in ways that are formative. So Jeff makes sure that whatever subject is being taught is accompanied by hands-on experiential learning. These experiences take the learner deeper into the meaning of what is being taught by engaging the senses and placing some form of activity at the heart of the educational process.

A new kind of youth ministry recognizes the importance of providing holistic experiential learning opportunities for our youth. If we are going to be intentional about developing followers of Jesus and guiding them along the way, then we must be committed to learning techniques that go beyond mechanical repetition.

Attribute 5: A learner-centered environment seeks to help students learn with and through one another.

When learning environments are built around the curriculum or the teacher, students tend to learn in isolation from one another. The instructor provides all the input and each student takes in what he or she can. But educational systems that limit interaction between students can hinder their development. A learner-centered environment creates opportunities for students to learn from one another.

I used to hate when my tenth-grade biology teacher would assign me a partner that was either a pain or a brain. I would much rather have done extra work myself to accomplish the task than be forced to work with someone else. Sharing responsibilities wasn't the easy way to arrive at the desired destination. You had to coordinate who was doing what part of the project and when you were going to get together to discuss the progress, and your grade at the end of the project was partially dependent on another person's efforts. I hated it. I especially hated it when the person I was partnered with was smarter than I am. At that time, my self-esteem couldn't handle that. I would have greatly preferred to work in isolation over working collaboratively with another student.

As I look back on those years, I realize that this particular teacher wasn't trying to wreck my self-esteem or burden me unnecessarily with the responsibility of working with someone else. She was actually teaching me the value of learning along with and from someone else. She knew that the abilities to work and learn collaboratively were critical life skills I would need in the future. Today, as the president of a national organization, I lean on learning and operating in collaboration rather than isolation.

Collaborative learning environments are healthy for all students. While some of your youth may not desire to study or uncover important truths alongside others, your teaching them how to work together is critical to their personal faith as well as our faith globally. A new kind of youth ministry is strategic about creating collaborative learning environments.

Attribute 6: A learner-centered environment emphasizes process over product.

One other challenging trend I've observed in many North American youth ministries is that their educational efforts tend to be more concerned with the product than the process. Why do we assume we have to have a completely made disciple by the time our students graduate high school? Why do we spend so much time thinking about the "end product?" No follower of Jesus is ever a finished product. Philippians 3:12 reminds us that we are not yet perfect, but urged to "press on" to the calling of Christ. Rather than strategizing our entire ministry around producing a model follower of Jesus, I contend it is much more helpful to realize that each of our young people is on a journey with Christ. We don't determine the end product, but we can heavily influence the process or passage the developing follower of Jesus has embraced and is navigating through.

A youth ministry focused on product seeks to equip teenagers with all the answers for a life in the way of Jesus. How ridiculous is it for our churches and leaders to think that any person in their adolescent years can be made a fully devoted follower of Jesus? Equally ridiculous is the effort to think that any of us, regardless of age, can be made into fully devoted followers of Jesus. What would it be like if churches—or more specifically youth ministries—sought to invite students into a developing process of following Jesus? I contend that we would have more people who are continually seeking to live, love, and lead like Jesus.

A process-driven youth ministry seeks only to give tools to discover a life in the way of Jesus. Too often we teach as if we have already found all the answers required for a life in the way of Jesus. How could an infinite, immutable, immense God be all figured out by humanity? It can't! So why are we creating learning environments designed to make a product rather than learning environments designed to guide through a process? It just doesn't make sense.

A new kind of youth ministry attempts to guide students in an ongoing process of discovering God and stops trying to graduate students who have it all figured out. A new kind of youth ministry stops panicking about the product being made and starts rejoicing in the process or passage being traveled.

Discovering the most effective educational environment for developing followers of Christ is a difficult task. You may not be in a position to immediately change all you are doing currently in teaching followers of Jesus—and it would probably be foolish for you to try. Pick one or two of the above attributes and try implementing them slowly. Be sure you understand your ministry context, as it plays a critical role in determining the most effective educational methods to use.

FOR REFLECTION AND DISCUSSION:

- What is the difference between learner-centered and teacher-centered education?

- Are the educational elements of your ministry designed around the needs of the students or the preferences and skills of the teacher?

- Are you looking for opportunities to evolve in your methods? Are you allowing your techniques to grow and change?

- Does pressure to cover a lot of ground in your teaching prevent you from going deeper? If so, how can you adjust this?

- What kind of experiential learning experiences does your ministry offer its students? How do you involve students in one another's learning?

- Are you more concerned about the process of spiritual growth or the final product?

8 RECULTURING OURSELVES

The Youth Worker's Journey of Personal Transformation

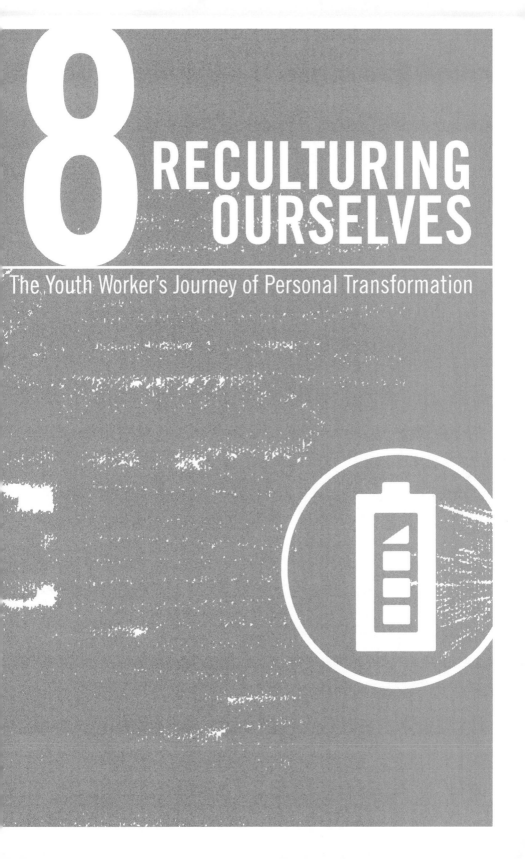

In my role as president of Sonlife Ministries, I have the opportunity and privilege to travel throughout North America and interact with youth workers in a variety of different contexts. The opportunity to learn about and from others is one of the more enjoyable aspects of my job.

When I arrive in a new city for a speaking engagement, training, or consultation, I'm often picked up at the airport by the youth pastor or one of the volunteer youth workers from the church I'm visiting. Typically, we go to lunch or dinner, I am welcomed into their home, and we stay up late drinking beer or coffee and talking. The other days of my trip often end similarly, with long informal conversations about their church and youth ministry in general. By the time I head back to the airport a few days later, I've had the chance to get to know the youth worker who is hosting me fairly well. One can really get to know the habits and customs of another person by living with them for three to five days. I wouldn't say that my host and I always become great friends, since time and distance limit our interactions. But we do form a relationship that often grows over time.

After nearly three years of traveling between eight and fifteen days a month, I have gotten to know several dozen youth pastors. I probably exchange a monthly e-mail with about half of those folks, meet up with them at conventions or conferences, and in some cases I am invited back to their area for further training or consulting—only now it us under the auspices of a growing relationship.

These travel and training opportunities have allowed me to make some observations about youth pastors. Some of the characteristics I've seen in them serve as healthy reminders for me, especially as they relate to things like shepherding students, managing conflict, communicating truth, and casting a vision. But there are other qualities I've observed among many youth pastors that are unhealthy and certainly not worth imitating.

The simple fact is that we youth workers are all human. In fact, much about the state of youth ministry today can be attributed to the fact that every youth pastor is a particular mix of strengths and weaknesses. Each youth worker I meet in my travels is a combination of good and godly characteristics as well as imperfections and shortcomings.

I'd like to share some of my observations about the particular strengths and weaknesses that seem most common among those who have felt called into youth ministry. Often, these gifts and imperfections are interrelated. It's my hope that by becoming aware of these tendencies, and by seeking to build on the positives and transform the troublesome areas, we can offer the kind of leadership that the church needs for youth ministry in the twenty-first century.

OBSERVING THE NORTH AMERICAN YOUTH WORKER

Observation 1: Youth workers are both steadfast and lazy people.

Do you know anyone you'd describe as steadfast? Such persons are reliable, firm, unwavering, and loyal. Steadfast people have a resolve that allows them to face the toughest situations with remarkable amounts of dependence on God, self-control, and poise. It takes an awful lot to shake people who are steadfast. They are human, after all, so there will be times when particular events or situations in life will cause them to stop in their tracks. But usually they are soon able to shake it off and move on. Admittedly, such people are sometimes so able to keep going through even the most difficult circumstances that they may move on too fast and never allow themselves to lament. I guess that's part of what makes them human...

I have a friend and former coworker who reminds me of what it means to be steadfast. Eric recently left Sonlife after working with us here for more than fifteen years. While working for our ministry which seeks to serve churches throughout North America, Eric also committed a ton of time and energy to volunteer in the youth ministry of a local church. Eric is always on time to a meeting or appointment; finishes the work he starts; stays poised in challenging situations; makes decisions with clarity, confidence, and few second guesses; and most of all has a committed prayer life like no one else I have ever seen. A new kind of youth ministry needs more youth workers who show that kind of steadfastness and dedication.

On the contrary, a new kind of youth ministry needs to purge from its core the laziness that in too many cases far outweighs the steadfastness. I am constantly running into youth workers who are unwilling to do any extra work that might inconvenience them in some way. I have very little tolerance for lazy people who are unwilling to make an effort—especially when such laziness shapes their ministries.

A few weeks ago I received a call from a senior pastor who was concerned about her youth pastor's work ethic. She told me that this youth pastor is always late, seldom comes prepared, lacks initiative, reacts lethargically to tasks given, and calls in sick two or three times a month. Knowing that I had a growing friendship with this youth pastor, the senior pastor asked me, "What should I do with him? I have talked with him about this on several different occasions and the Session has spoken to him regarding his work efforts. I just don't know what to do. Can you meet with him?" I told her that I was no motivational guru or counselor, but that I'd be glad to meet with him and see if I could determine what was up.

A few days later, I met with this youth pastor for coffee and we talked. When I asked if he knew why I wanted to talk with him, he said "Yeah. My pastor thinks I am lazy, and she wants you to try and pump me up."

It took me awhile to get to the core issue. I asked him if he respected the senior pastor, or if he had some lack of confidence in her. He responded, "No, I think she is great. She is a wonderful pastor."

I asked if he thought he was paid enough, if he was questioning his call, if he liked his job. None of those were the problem. I then asked, "Is there something within you—like fear or doubt or a lack of confidence—that makes you behave lazily?" He responded that there might be something, but he really wasn't sure what.

So I asked my final question, "So, what is the deal, bro?"

He responded with, "I don't know. I guess I just don't want to work. I mean, I love hanging out with the kids, but I just don't want to do the other garbage I have to do to hang out with them."

I offered him the old saying, "We do what we don't want to do, in order to do the things we love." It went right over his head.

I still talk with this youth pastor occasionally. He has moved across town to another church, where he is having the same kind of experience.

It wouldn't be such a big deal if he were the only lazy youth pastor I'd ever met. The tragic part is I can name a couple dozen folks like that who love "hanging out with kids" but have little interest in doing the hard work that makes for an effective ministry. Some of the harshest words in Scripture are directed at slothfulness—the biblical word for laziness.

So what do we do with lazy youth workers? Do we just write them off? Are they no good to God? Well, I would never say that anyone is no good to God, but there may be some folks who are no good in youth ministry. Yet there are many others who simply need the support of other youth workers who are steadfast to surround them and encourage them to change their patterns.

A new kind of youth ministry cannot afford lazy youth workers. Do you think you are lazy? Don't ask yourself—we seldom see ourselves as clearly as others can. Ask a friend, a real friend—one who will tell you the truth. And if you determine that you are lazy, do something about it.

It's worth mentioning that overwork is also a problem among some youth workers. Many youth pastors work too much—and can never slow down, rest, and spend time with their families and friends. This, too, is a problem that needs to be addressed. If our lives do not include a balance of rest and recreation in addition to our work, we run the risk of burning out or breaking down.

Observation 2: Youth workers are both happy for and envious of others.

Do you struggle with envy? I do. Everyone else's skills and gifts always look better than mine. And often it seems like others are in much better situations, and success comes easily to them. I am always comparing my abilities and achievements to those of other people. It is a challenge for me to be happy for others. I am working to purge myself of this sin—but it is constant work.

My friend Seth is an amazing communicator. In fact, he might be the best communicator to high school students I've ever heard. The only reason you probably haven't heard of Seth is because he couldn't care less about getting into the "national spotlight." I think that is one of the things that makes him such a good communicator.

I am always comparing myself to Seth. Deep inside I know I'm not as good a communicator as he is, and that makes me jealous and keeps me from celebrating his gifts. Some time (any time!) I wish he would stumble on a word, lose his train of thought, misread his notes—or just trip coming up on stage! Why do I wish that on him? Because I'd like to be as good as he is, but I'm not—and I probably never will be. I should be okay with that—but often I'm not.

We are all in youth ministry because we care about kids. We want to see young people grow in their relationship with God. When we hear of other youth workers and churches that are making that happen, we should celebrate the ways that God is working in and through them. And in our best moments, that is exactly what we do. But many youth workers are jealous people. We are not always happy for those among us who "make it to the big time." We wish we were the ones getting the recognition, so instead of offering encouragement and praise, we are often unsupportive, and sometimes even openly critical, of those who get the attention we crave.

I have a friend who has been in youth ministry for over a decade. He is a very talented and highly regarded youth pastor. His students think the world of him, the parents respect him, and fellow youth pastors look to him for support and wisdom. He has always served in medium-sized churches, and is forever applying for that "big" job in a megachurch. He wants a bigger budget, a team to lead, a bus driver, his own youth room, etc. But for some reason God has placed him in small-to-medium-sized churches. So when another youth pastor gets the "big" job in that megachurch, my friend cannot be happy for that person. He doesn't go out of his way to be hurtful or discouraging, but he wrestles with saying, "Good for you. That's great! Congratulations!" (Maybe my friend doesn't realize that being in a big church can be a big pain in the neck at times!)

In order for us to clear the way for a new kind of youth ministry to emerge, we need to purge ourselves of such destructive envy. We need to become happy for one another, and celebrate the ways God is working in others' ministries. We need to stop continually comparing ourselves with one another. God has given us all different gifts and uses us all in different ways—and this is a good thing! Let's own that, stop all our comparing, and let God use the "me" he created!

Observation 3: Youth workers are dedicated to and undedicated to students.

My wife and I were out for dinner one night during a time when we were trying to discern the next step of where God was leading us. We were wrestling with several possibilities that would have taken me out of hands-on youth ministry—including becoming a senior pastor, church planting, running a small business, and even managing a coffee shop. She asked me, "Do you love students?"

Quickly and emphatically I responded, "Of course I do!"

"Really?" she said. "I think you love the 'ministry' part of youth ministry a whole lot more than you love the 'youth' part of youth ministry."

After reflecting on that statement for a while (and eating a few more raviolis), I decided she was right. I'd fallen in love with the peripheral activity and buzz that surrounded ministry to youth. I had fallen in love with strategy, leadership development, problem solving, efficiency implementation, directing a team and the recognition that came with all of that. But somewhere along the line, I'd stopped loving what had drawn me into youth ministry in the first place. Somehow, I had stopped loving students. I cared about them, prayed for them at times, went to their games and activities, went to the hospital to visit them, and so on. But those were all just part of the job—they no longer were flowing out of a genuine love for the young people in my care.

Eventually, I came to the realization that I no longer loved students all that much. And the biggest reason why was because I really didn't love God all that much either. I have noticed that as I have recovered my passion to find union with God, my love for people—especially students—has returned.

When I think about love for students, I think of Jim Newberry. I met Jim a few years ago. He is currently a youth pastor in the Kansas City area, and has been in youth ministry for more than 15 years. Jim has often pushed me to think about the future of youth ministry, and he's a big supporter of the emergent movement—not because it is trendy, fun, or interesting, or even because it is perceived to be associated with people who deconstruct and rethink everything. He supports the emergent movement because he genuinely thinks, like many others, that it is absolutely what the church needs to love God and love others in a deeper way.

Jim loves people. He has compassion for others like I have never seen before. His passion for and devotion to students oozes out of him. You cannot help but notice it, and there is no denying it is authentic. Jim has given his life to serving youth and their families, and he does it well. He may not always be a youth pastor but he will always express God's love to the heart of others. That practice of loving others is embedded in him.

The church needs more youth workers who love students with the kind of passion Jim does. Unfortunately, I run into too many youth workers who are a lot like I was. They love all that surrounds youth ministry, but have either forgotten how or decided not to love students anymore. This is a problem. Youth pastors who don't love students anymore should go do something else with their lives and time. We have to commit ourselves to falling in love with our students again—every day. A new kind of youth ministry is one that is very intentional about expressing the heart of God to the hearts of others—and the heart of God loves unfailingly and unchangingly.

Observation 4: Youth workers are learners and know-it-alls.

Do you know any youth workers who seem to think they know everything? I sure do. I run into them all the time—and they are easy for me to recognize, because I used to be one of them. "Hi, my name is Chris, and I think I know everything." A couple of my friends used to make me say that phrase whenever we sat down to talk. At some point in my life, I began believing I knew all there was to know about youth ministry. I am not sure why—maybe because I'd made it to the "big time." What a joke! Anyway, since coming to the realization that I really don't know all that much about youth ministry, I've become a learner. I try hard to read two ministry-related books a week, read blogs, listen to people speak on subjects related to the church and youth ministry specifically, and do my best to study others in action. I feel like I have come to a place of real learning.

Not long ago, 9,000 people gathered in Nashville for the annual youth ministry convention sponsored by Youth Specialties. A record number of people came together for several days of seminars, work-shops, concerts, and motivational talks. But I wonder how many of the folks at that convention sat listening to one of the terrific pre-senters there and said (or thought), "Well, no kidding, of course you would do that" or "It doesn't take a rocket scientist to figure that out" or "I could lead a better workshop than this." I was amazed at another recent Youth Specialties convention in Pittsburgh, when the person seated next to me at a workshop turned to me and said, "This guy says the same stuff every year. When is he going to come up with something new? I have been coming for five years, and it is always the same old stuff from this idiot!"

"You've been coming to this convention for five years, and you have attended this workshop all five years?" I asked.

"Yep" he cynically and proudly said.

I responded by saying, "Well, then who is the *real* idiot here?" He got the point. I know he got the point because he grabbed his conference saddlebag full of free goodies and got up and walked out. He was just one of the many youth workers I've come into contact with over my travels who think they could do not only the speaker's job, but mine and yours as well!

Life-long learning is a very familiar term. Nearly every post-secondary educational institution provides some form of continu-ing education. Every day there seem to be more and more creative options for long-distance learning presented to the public. I can name a dozen or so colleges or universities that provide an ad-vanced degree in a field of study related to youth ministry. Most of them try to provide such education at a discounted rate, or at least seek to make it as affordable as possible.

But life-long learning is not just about pursuing an advanced degree or continuing education credits in a formal setting. Life-long learning can also happen through mentors. Someone once heard me complaining about not having a mentor and told me, "Open your eyes! Look around you. There are people everywhere that you can learn from!" Not long after that I asked a seasoned youth worker who was a husband, father of three, and a successful business owner to mentor me. In many ways I've found that I'm just beginning my education.

One of my mentors is named Klaas. When I was living near Minneapolis, Klaas and I met weekly for several hours at a time. We were very serious about these meeting times, meeting just about every week for nearly two years. My time with Klaas wasn't just about gaining more intellectual knowledge. It was more about learning how to live in the ways of Jesus—learning how to be a better husband, father, youth pastor, friend, neighbor, servant leader, and citizen. Since I moved to Chicago, we are no longer able to meet face-to-face each week, but we do regularly stay in touch via e-mail and phone. When I travel back to Minneapolis, I make it a point to connect with Klaas.

AUTHENTIC LEADERSHIP, INC.
Dan Webster
www.authenticleadershipinc.com

Authentic Leadership, Inc. exists to train and inspire leaders to live in ways that have great impact. ALI's founder, Dan Webster, believes leaders who want to make a difference over the long haul must understand and develop both their inner and outer worlds. Like many of my friends, I can testify to the impact that ALI's training and LifePlan has had in nurturing my own leadership skills. If you need help moving closer to who God wants you to be as a leader, then connect with Dan Webster and Authentic Leadership.

For every know-it-all I meet in youth ministry, I meet other youth workers who desire to learn. These learners understand that they will never be finished products. They understand that being "right" isn't nearly as important as continually pursuing the ways of God. They seek to gather all the knowledge they can, hoping to use it in some way for the glory of God.

In talking about the mentoring relationship between teacher and student, Brian McLaren sometimes talks about the way the great violin maker Stradivarius would relate to his apprentices. Brian poses the question, "How did Stradivarius' students know how to make a violin just like he did?

Did he write a 'how-to' manual and leave it for them just before he passed away?" The answer, of course, is "No." Stradivarius' students were able to make world-class violins even after the master was gone because he had taken the time and effort to teach his apprentices everything he had come to understand about crafting violins. Brian says Stradivarius took his students to search for the perfect wood. They would pick up the pieces of wood, determine their density, smell them for age, rub them for texture, and continue to do so until they found the perfect piece. He taught the correct hand position necessary for crafting the bow. He taught his apprentices everything he knew about making violins, and when he died, they continued to make the world's best violins in the way of Stradivarius.

Sounds just a bit like what Jesus did with his disciples, eh? And this is what Klaas continues to do for me. He shares with me all that he has come to learn about life, and all he is continuing to learn.

Do you have these kind of mentoring relationships with anyone? Whom are you learning from? Who is learning from you?

A new kind of youth ministry is more intentional about mentoring students and leaders. A new kind of youth ministry weeds out the know-it-alls and makes room for teachers who are continuing to learn, who are willing to take what they are discovering along life's journey and offer that wisdom to other travelers.

SEVEN TRAIL MARKERS ON YOUR JOURNEY FROM HERE TO THERE

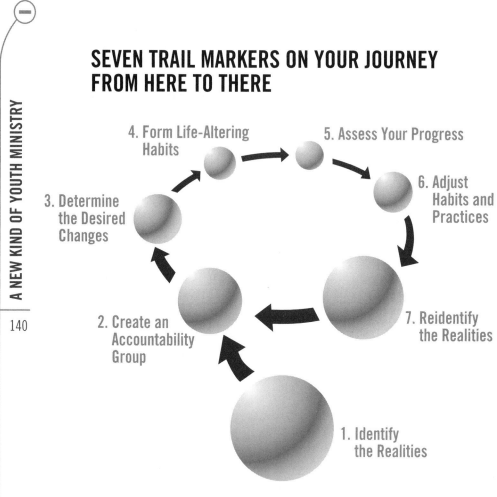

4. Form Life-Altering Habits

5. Assess Your Progress

6. Adjust Habits and Practices

3. Determine the Desired Changes

7. Reidentify the Realities

2. Create an Accountability Group

1. Identify the Realities

One of my first ministry positions was as an intern serving under my friend, Dave Michener. I remember how Dave used to tell his students, volunteer leaders, and staff, "It is okay to be wherever you are, it is just not okay to stay there."

I have probably repeated Dave's words a thousand times—to my own students, volunteer leaders, and interns, and perhaps most often to myself. When I feel stuck, complacent, or unmotivated to change, I repeat those words until I feel motivated to wake up and do something about changing myself. The first part of Dave's statement ("It is okay to be wherever you are…") acknowledges the reality of whatever place we may find ourselves, without giving us permission to stay in that place. The second part of Dave's statement ("...it is just not okay to stay there") is an encouragement to transform—to move forward, stretch, develop, and become something new.

Perhaps you've found yourself pictured in some of the negative qualities I've listed in the observations and descriptions of the North American youth worker above. If that is the case, how can you change? If you are lazy, unloving, envious, or a know-it-all (or if you struggle with some other trait that you know is harmful for your development), how will you move away from that and become the person you want to be? How will you get from *here* to *there*?

I've never met a single youth worker who comes to the realization of who they really are and then wants to remain in that place. But once we've discovered that where we are is not where we want to be, how do we begin to make that journey?

If you are a walker, horseback rider, biker, or hiker, you know that most pathways have markers along the way. These markers are designed to guide you on your journey, and often provide helpful information such as potential dangers, resting areas, and campsites along the way. For the purposes of helping you get from "here" to "there," let me suggest seven trail markers that can help you as you discover and navigate your trek.

Trail Marker 1: Identify the Realities

Identifying your current reality is a critical starting point. Before you can begin to see change in your life, you have to come to grips with who you really are and where you are headed. There are a number of ways to identify these realties. You might journal a month of your life, and then use that to determine where and how you spend your time and energy. Perhaps you could take a formal self-inventory like the well-known DISC or StengthFinder. You might even take a personal retreat and ask God to help you more clearly see who you are and what you are becoming. I find that taking a pipe full of my favorite tobacco out to a log in the woods helps me in my own process of self-reflection. It really doesn't matter what process you use to identify the current realities of your life—just find a comfortable (or uncomfortable) way to do it, and make it happen.

Trail Marker 2: Create an Accountability Group

After you've identified your current situation, your next step should be to form an accountability group of two to four persons. This group will serve to affirm the realities you've identified (or challenge them) and will later hold you accountable for the changes you decide to make.

This group should be comprised of people you trust who desire to see a change in your life as much as you do. These people are given permission to be brutally honest and to speak into your life at any and all times. Without such a group, you'll be tempted to assume that everything is fine and that you have already reached the "there" in your life. Let your group help determine where you are on the journey—and support you as you move forward.

Trail Marker 3: Determine the Desired Changes

Once you've identified the realities and invited a group to help shape who you are becoming, you'll need to determine the changes you plan to make in order to become a different person tomorrow than you are today. Just pick two or three areas in your life where you want to grow. You cannot change everything overnight, so don't try. Be sure your accountability group knows what changes you desire to make, and then journey on to marker number four.

Trail Marker 4: Form Life-Altering Habits

This midpoint of the journey may very well be the key to this whole process. So work with your accountability group to determine habits that will help you to move from "here" to "there." These habits are not necessarily just traditional Christian practices. They might very well be simple lifestyle adjustments that will help you discover helpful Christian practices for your development down the road.

Let me illustrate what I mean by talking about my own adjustment. After identifying the realities of my life and establishing an accountability group, I determined in step 3 that a primary change I needed to make was to become more patient, more selfless, and less cross with other people. I then had to begin forming habits that would help me move toward those goals. My accountability group and I brainstormed a list of ways I could begin to make the changes I was seeking. We determined that, in order to become more patient, I would—

- wait in the longest checkout line at the grocery store.

- choose the longest line at the highway toll booth.

- let someone else go ahead of me to get their haircut.

- wait in the longest line at the airport security checkpoint.

- wait behind another car for refueling at the gas station, even if the other pumps are vacant.

- wait in the drive-through line at McDonalds even if no one is standing in line inside.

To help me become more selfless, I would—

- give away at least one of the Christmas presents I receive each year.

- pray simple prayers like, "Not my will, but thine, O God" or "Let your will be done".

- sit in the back seat of a car while traveling with others even if I have the largest frame of anyone in the vehicle.

- stop mentally dividing the number of slices in a pizza hoping I'll get the extra one.

LIVE IT FORWARD
Kent Julian
www.liveitforward.com

Live It Forward™ exists to inspire and equip individuals to dream more, be more, and achieve more in the most important areas of life. The ministry focuses on empowering young people (teenagers, college students, and young professionals) to develop L.I.F.E. leadership skills (Life-long learning, Integrity, Focus, Everyday Actions) that will help them pursue their dreams and calling. Live it Forward can help you become who God wants you to be. If you are ready for your life to move from ordinary to extraordinary, then connect with Kent Julian and Live It Forward.

To help me manage my anger and be less cross with others, I would-

- carry prayer beads in my pocket, so that when I get angry, I can simply rub the cross with my thumb and forefinger.

- count 10 breaths when irritated before I responded to someone else.

- try hard not to knit my eyebrows or shake my head in disgust.

- speak more softly to someone when upset.

These are simple habits, and you won't find them in any book of spiritual disciplines or Christian practices. They are, however, practices I've adopted as part of my own Christian discipleship because they help me in my desire to increase the frequency of the holy moments in my life.

Trail Marker 5: Assess Your Progress

As you move forward in your journey, it is critical that you take stock of the progress you are making. Enlist the help of your accountability group to join you in evaluating how well you are doing. Don't be discouraged if you have not completely mastered the new behavior you desire; progress is really what it is all about.

Trail Marker 6: Adjust Habits and Practices

After assessing your progress, adjust your habits as needed. Perhaps you've found that you're not finding opportunities to practice your chosen habits in the everyday life situations that unfold around you. At this point, you may need to rethink what kind of habits will really bring forth change in your life. You must be sure that the habits you've chosen are ones you can practice regularly, allowing you to maximize your potential for life change.

Trail Marker 7: Reidentify the Realities

After a chosen season of time, gather again with your accountability group and determine if you are a changing person. How are you progressing in the areas that you identified as most in need of growth? Where do you most see a need for further development? As you identify your new reality, the journey of transformation begins anew.

The goal is to continue to make progress in becoming all that God desires for us to be. My guess is that if you work hard at crafting life change through a process (whether it is the one proposed here or another), you will be on your way to getting from "here" to "there" as a developing follower of Jesus, a wife or husband, a mother or father, a youth worker, a friend or a neighbor.

A new kind of youth ministry is comprised of youth workers who desire to reculture not only their ministry practices but their entire lives. As we discover new life in the ways of Jesus, God's creative Spirit will flow afresh through us, enlivening our lives and our ministries.

FOR REFLECTION AND DISCUSSION:

- Personal Assessment: Place a mark on the line to indicate where you see yourself on each of the following scales.

STEADFAST   LAZY

HAPPY FOR OTHERS   ENVIOUS OF OTHERS

DEDICATED   UNDEDICATED

LEARNER   KNOW-IT-ALL

- Do you have a mentor? If not, whom could you ask to serve as your mentor?

- Whom are you mentoring?

9 MAKING IT HAPPEN

How Do We Get from Old to New?

We've talked throughout this book about the need for a new kind of youth ministry. We've considered how the needs of today's youth are often going unmet by the established practices within the field of youth ministry. If we hope to have an impact on the youth of this generation, it is essential that our ministries reculture their approaches in key areas like evangelism, discipleship, mission, and education.

But at some point we have to move from conversing about change to implementing it. Change doesn't just happen by itself—at least intentional and effective change doesn't. Sure, if we wait long enough, change will occur—but chances are it won't be the kind of change that delivers positive outcomes. Therefore, it becomes a leadership priority to move beyond dreaming and idea generation to implementing a new vision of ministry. In other words, the task of initiating and leading our ministries through the process of change rests squarely upon our shoulders. This chapter lays out a simple process that will help you plan and then guide your ministry through the passage from "old" to "new."

LISTEN CAREFULLY

Listening is the critical first step of the journey. I've always been fascinated by how ships and submarines use sonar for navigation. Sonar (which is an acronym for Sound, Navigation and Ranging) helps traveling sea vessels determine the position of underwater objects by transmitting sound waves and then measuring the time it takes for their echo to return. This method of listening provides a picture of the surrounding environment, highlighting potential obstacles and providing the necessary information for safe passage.

Careful listening can help us guide our ministries on the path of change and negotiate the obstacles that might prevent us from journeying toward a new kind of youth ministry. When one sets out to lead change, it's common for "unseen objects" that might otherwise go unnoticed to block the path. Differing philosophies and convictions, relational components, others' contentions and values, ministry paradigms, public opinion, personal preferences and style, political power plays, leadership weaknesses, and a slew of other contextual realities can prevent us from making the changes necessary to move from old to new. It is imperative that we have a process that maintains our complete awareness.

Before you can begin to execute your desired change, you need to take time to listen for answers to the following questions:

- What is God saying?

- What is your heart saying?

- What is your supervisor saying?

- What are those around you (like your volunteers) saying?

Listening is a skill that many leaders need significant help mastering. Most leaders are so quick to develop a vision and proceed with the nuts and bolts of moving forward that they neglect to ask the right questions. Just as a ship emits sound pulses to determine its context, you need to be sure you are absolutely aware of the contextual realities before launching into a reculturing process. Is God calling you to reculture your ministry? What is your heart telling you to do? What does your boss think about your plan? Is she going to be opposed to or bless your desired changes? Have you listened to others in ministry around you? What are others noticing about your ministry? Are others thinking change is needed, or do they believe everything is ideal as it is? You need to ask these questions, and collect accurate data. You need to become so fully aware of your surroundings and context that you are confident not only that reculturing is possible, but that it is enormously needed.

For the sake of your ministry (and I mean the people that comprise it, not the programs), do not launch into a reculturing process if you discover enough submerged objects that finding your way from old to new will bring irreparable damage to the "vessel." True change is never easy, and some degree of damage is to be expected in any process. But in some situations, the price of the change might be irreparable damage to your ongoing ministry.

DEVELOP A TEAM

After a season of listening well and collecting the necessary data about the potential obstacles, you'll want to establish a team that will oversee the transition process.

Whom are you inviting on this journey with you? What people will help you implement the desired change? Should that team include your senior pastor or boss? A few of your key volunteers? A few capable and willing parents? Some students? What team of people are you going to engage and employ to guide the passage from old to new?

I enjoy nothing more than being on a team. I have been on teams my whole life. I have been on sports teams, construction crews, mission teams, multiple-staff church situations, neighborhood watch teams, think tanks, conference-planning and student-event teams, and an assortment of other types of teams. I've found that the best thing about being on a team is that I'm never forced to rely solely on myself. Whether playing college basketball, building a house, or sailing, I have found confidence in the ability of those around me. I lean on others and want and expect others to lean on me. That is teaming—sharing the load.

If you are going to lead your ministry from old to new, you will need a team. Don't try to navigate the passage on your own. I don't care how long you've been at your church, or how much credibility you have or think you have—do not attempt to go about change by yourself. Instead, seek, develop, employ, and coach a team that is strong enough to help you accomplish your goals. Because reculturing is a contact sport, you can expect that, just as with athletic competitions, you will get knocked down, frustrated, tired, angry, and lazy. At those times of struggle, you'll need others around you to help you up, calm you, spell you, and motivate you. And in the good times, when you see the changes you'd hoped for occurring, you will want to celebrate those moments with your teammates as well.

Teaming can be hard work. At times you may feel like it'd be easier just to do it all yourself, and you may be tempted to do so. Resist the desire to lead on your own. You will never be successful in making lasting change if you try to go it alone.

CREATE A VISION

Do those around you sense the need for change? Can they grasp the benefits of reculturing the ministry? Are those around you fully aware of the opportunities and potential results of such change? Do others involved with your ministry, especially your change team, have an image of change in their mind? Are others' hearts engaged in your mission? Are you articulating the reason why things need to be different? Are you helping people see the future?

If you want to successfully navigate the passage from old to new, you will need an unmistakable, crisp, and gripping vision that will compel people and draw them in. You will need a common cause. You will need to articulate a vision that people can not only embrace but also endorse.

Think back on your life. Who have you known that was able to convince you of the need for change? Have you known people who were not only charismatic enough to lead but were able to give you a compelling reason to drop what you were doing to join them?

Growing up, I had a friend who could always convince me to help him with just about any chore. He talked me into helping him shovel his driveway, take the garbage out, rake leaves, clean the pool, and wash his car. He always made things sound so exciting and fun. He also made things sound so needed. The faster we raked the leaves, the faster we could ride our bikes. The sooner we got the garbage out to the side of the road, the sooner we could shoot hoops. The quicker we cleaned his room, the quicker we could play video games. The faster I helped him clean the pool, the faster we could jump in and get wet! My friend was the master at casting a vision.

As I look back on our childhood friendship, I realize that part of what made me help my friend with his household chores was who he was as a person—genuine, charismatic, fun. But even more important than that was the persuasive reason he would give me each and every time he requested my help. He always made the task seem so purposeful and important. I never once remember thinking or saying, "You're crazy! Clean your own room." I only ever remember saying to myself, "Yeah. You're right. As soon as we get that done, we can be riding our bikes!" My friend got me to help him partly because he always convinced me there was something in it for me. Maybe it was cooling off on a hot day by jumping into the deep end of his pool or playing the video games that I didn't have at my house. Whatever the reason, my helping him also benefited me. But the other reason I would help him is because I love working for and with others. Call me gullible, but I think if my childhood friend were to call me up today and ask for my help, I would do it. His vision always captivates me.

CHART THE COURSE

Okay, so you have listened to the sounds and voices of those around you, built a team to help you lead change, and cast a vision. Now what? Well, you and your team need to chart the course you intend to travel. You will need to plot your schedule,

THE RIDDLE GROUP
Mark Riddle
www.theriddlegroup.com

The Riddle Group offers consulting and support that helps build sustainable youth ministries. Their mission is to expand the kingdom of God by helping leaders, youth workers, and parents create healthy environments for ministry to adolescents and their families. Through their training, you'll be given the lenses to see the assumptions, patterns of behavior, and expectations about staff, programs, mission, and congregation that can often cause ministries to struggle. The Riddle group can help you navigate the difficult and ever-changing waters as you journey toward a new kind of youth ministry.

create an itinerary, and set a direction. How will you reach your preferred future? What needs to happen to reach your goals? What are your next steps and who on the team is going to do what? How will you track progress or evaluate your effectiveness?

I am not a big fan of just hopping into the car and going for a drive. With today's fuel prices, I need to know where I'm going and what the best way is to get there. I need a course or a direction. I am not creative or free-spirited enough to jump in the car and let my "inner voice" tell me what turn to take next. Additionally, I'm too "clock conscious" to just go out for a drive with no real plan for how I'll get where I'm going.

Chances are, most of your team will also want a plan to follow in guiding your ministry through a process of change. As you set out to reculture from old to new, you'll want to develop what I call a Ministry Action Plan (MAP) that will help lay out your basic timeline and steps for implementing change. Your MAP can help guide you, keep you and your team focused, project the times for various changes, and track your progress. Don't feel the need to create this plan on your own; instead, lean on your team.

Although creating a plan is important, remember to listen for the guidance of the Holy Spirit as you consider each step you will take. As you follow the Spirit's leading, your MAP can enable you to be most effective in stewarding your time and resources.

SET SAIL

I think many of the best inventions have never been seen because they remain in the minds and hearts of people. As far as we have come in innovation and technology, I still believe we are a long way from being all "invented out." I think a lot of potentially great ideas remain locked away in the minds and hearts of people because they are afraid to push off from shore. People are scared of the process of moving to something new and different, so they convince themselves that they are content with the old. Therefore, many of the best ideas never get developed. It is tragic, really.

If you are going to reculture, if you are going to pass from the old into the new, you will have to set sail. You can gather data and listen to others' thoughts until you have no more room to store them. You can build a team, develop and cast a compelling vision, set the intended direction—and never go anywhere. In order to lead change, you can't just gather everyone together and board the ship while it stays as the dock. Eventually, you must push off and set sail.

Do not think you have to make it a fast journey. Once you've determined that the reculturing process is something God wants you to do, I'd recommend that you and your team pick just three or four new ideas and practices that you are going to implement in the next year. Don't try to overhaul your entire ministry in six months. Begin with smaller steps, assuming that it might take several years to create a culture of change.

Maybe over the next year, rather than rethinking all your educational efforts, you might simply try to rework just one of your educational programs so it is more learner-centered. Or you might leave most of your traditional outreach events in place, and just drop one or two of them in order to give more attention to helping your students understand and live out life-dynamic evangelism. Perhaps you will simply set sail with a personal goal of trying to get out of the way this next year so that the leadership of those around you can flourish. Or maybe you will dedicate yourself to affirming students as they dream big, instead of telling them all of the reasons they won't make their dreams reality. Whatever steps you might decide on, be sure to take your time and enjoy the journey. Don't feel like you have to rework every part of your ministry next month. If you do rush, you might find that your efforts do more harm than good.

TRACK PROGRESS AND MAKE ADJUSTMENTS

As you move forward in the reculturing process, it is essential to determine what kind of progress you are making and then make the necessary adjustments to the process. Not too far into the reculturing process it is critical to evaluate your progress. How well is it going? Are we seeing successes? Is your team still following you? Is the vision compelling enough? Are people "getting" it?

Evaluating our own work is hard on a number of levels. Besides the fact that we may be too close to the situation to see it clearly, we may also be unwilling to face the difficult realities that emerge in our assessment. For example, in the process of writing this book, I've received lots of feedback on the manuscript from my editor and others who offered comments, questions, and suggestions. When I've received e-mails with edits and suggested changes, I've sometimes waited for days before opening the file. I didn't want to face the possibility that others might not think as highly of my ideas as I do. I wasn't sure I wanted to face the criticism—no matter how constructive. I wasn't comfortable with the idea that someone else might think my book stinks.

Evaluating can reveal weaknesses, highlight mistakes, point blame, reveal the truth, and uncover realities that we may not want to face. It can even crush you to the point of feeling paralyzed. But the truth of the matter, as we all know, is that if we don't take time to evaluate our progress, we may proceed in a direction that is not helpful, and may even be harmful. Your reculturing team must plan early on that it will face the realities. Developing a system of ongoing evaluation is critical to the success of your passage from old to new.

Evaluating can also be a positive way of marking the progress you are making. If you do not slow down long enough to evaluate your progress, you may miss the opportunity to celebrate the accomplishments. Celebrating your successes is as critical as uncovering your weakness. What team doesn't celebrate a victory? For the sake of team morale and the overall success of the reculturing process, it is vital to employ an evaluation system that allows your team to rally around its victories. A celebration, however small or seemingly insignificant, can build confidence and generate momentum—two ingredients to a winning team.

ASSESS YOUR OWN LEADERSHIP

Early in my ministry, I had time to coach sports. I coached basketball, soccer, baseball, and golf in several different high schools. My teams had some successes. We won games, tournaments, and even city championships. Contributing to the successes of those teams were a host of other coaches who helped me in areas where I had limited experience or skills. For example, as a golf coach, I understand the basics of a golf swing and could help my athletes improve. But some of my players reached a point where I could no longer help them. While I could teach the basics, when it came to the technicalities of refining their swing so they could shave further strokes off a scorecard, I was extremely limited in my ability to help. So I concentrated on what I could teach, and then borrowed the coaching ability of others to take my golfers to the next level. A good coach knows his or her limits.

The same is true whether you are leading a company, a school, a nonprofit, or a church. All of us have a ceiling to our scope and effectiveness as leaders. Most of us don't want to admit that our leadership ability has limits. Likewise, each one of us knows that there are people around us who can lead more effectively. The best leaders rely on the leadership of others to take our organizations to the next level. We certainly do not stop learning and developing our abilities, but we know enough when to recruit the help of others who are stronger and more effective.

As you travel the passage from old to new, you should spend extensive time evaluating yourself as a leader. What are your strengths? What are your growth areas? What are your limits? Can you call on others to lead in areas where you are weaker? Answers to questions like these might point toward more investigative questions like: Am I the right person to lead the ministry through the next phase of reculturing? Is it time for me to pass the baton? If so, to whom?

You may be the right person to lead your ministry through the process of change, but not the best person to maintain the effort until more change is needed. You may be the person to lead a ministry through a more stable period, but not the person to lead the next chapter in change. Knowing your limits is critical to the process. Be sure not to attempt more than you can do. If you do, you may be risking the success of the entire reculturing process.

Like a ship which uses sonar continually throughout its journey, keep your ears open as you implement and execute change, listening to the sounds and voices of those around you, and the call of the Spirit. Navigate the passage carefully, keeping your dependence on God, and your motivations as pure as possible. Know your limits, rely on your team, and be as clever as you can in drawing on the leadership of others. The journey toward a new kind of youth ministry will not be easy, but it is rewarding—not only for you as a leader, but for all the lives that will be touched by your ministry.

FOR REFLECTION AND DISCUSSION:

- Is this the right time for a significant reculturing of your ministry? Why or why not?

- With regard to your ministry and its effectiveness, what are you hearing from the voices around you? What are you hearing from students? From parents? From other staff and church leaders? From the Holy Spirit?

- List ten changes you would like to see in your youth ministry.

1.

2.

3.

4.

5.

6.

7.

8.

9.

10.

- What are three areas of your ministry that most need reculturing at this time?

1.

2.

3.

- How are you going to go about the reculturing process? What is your first step? And the next step? And the step after that?...

- How will you incorporate a process of ongoing assessment and evaluation into your reculturing efforts?

Contemplative Youth Ministry is a more organic approach to youth ministry, allowing you to create meaningful silence, foster covenant communities, engage students in contemplative activities, and maximize spontaneity—and to help your students recognize the presence of Jesus in their everyday lives.

Contemplative Youth Ministry
Practicing the Presence of Jesus

Mark Yaconelli

RETAIL $19.99
ISBN 0-310-26777-3

Visit **www.youthspecialties.com** or your local Christian bookstore.